Kelly Riddle is a budding author and a strong advocator for mental illness awareness. A seemingly average girl from a small town in rural Massachusetts, Kelly was changed forever by her near-death experience related to a five-year-long battle with anorexia and bulimia nervosa. *Noise* was written between the ages of 14 and 16 while Kelly was in high school, from which she graduated with a top position. She is 18 and in her freshman year of college at Northeastern University. There, she spends her free time mothering a happy-go-lucky Cavalier King Charles Spaniel puppy named Wednesday. And, as a Behavioural Neuroscience major, Kelly continues to pursue her passion for understanding and overcoming mental illness. She plans to continue writing and already has plans for following books.

To my therapist, Lindsay Brady, for helping me get better, and most importantly, to anorexia survivors everywhere.

Kelly Riddle

NOISE

AUSTIN MACAULEY PUBLISHERS™
LONDON • CAMBRIDGE • NEW YORK • SHARJAH

Ordering Information:
Quantity sales: special discounts are available on quantity purchases by corporations, associations, and others. For details, contact the publisher at the address below.

Publisher's Cataloging-in-Publication data
Riddle, Kelly
Noise

ISBN 9781641829328 (Paperback)
ISBN 9781641829335 (Hardback)
ISBN 9781645366454 (ePub e-book)

Library of Congress Control Number: 2019907902

The main category of the book — YOUNG ADULT NONFICTION / Social Topics / Eating Disorders & Body Image

www.austinmacauley.com/us

First Published (2019)
Austin Macauley Publishers LLC
40 Wall Street, 28th Floor
New York, NY 10005
USA
mail-usa@austinmacauley.com
+1 (646) 5125767

I would like to acknowledge my loving parents, David and Carol Riddle, for supporting me, both as a daughter and as an aspiring author. Bitter thanks are extended to all bullies, doctors, genes, and social media platforms which made this book possible in the first place by inciting my development of anorexia. Finally, all artwork is credited to Conor Toland of MassArt.

Contents

Kelly Riddle is a young woman, but she is wise far beyond her years. She was born and raised in a small town that nobody knows about, someplace deep in Massachusetts, yet somehow, *Ed*[1] still found her.

Broken into eight chapters, *Noise* follows Kelly in her battle against *Ed.* It all starts with a sort of **cycle**, featuring repeated, new, and scary emotions triggered by who-knows-what. Next, she steps back to examine her own **family** dynamics, also adjusting to Kelly's changing habits and expressions. Accordingly, she then steps outside the home and looks at **society** and its media-obsessed culture, unattainable body ideals, and more. On this note, the future feminist also includes a few special notes **to women**. Finally, the story transitions back to the individual in the chapter titled '**Freezing,**' which describes social factors that break and eventually freeze her heart—making her vulnerable to *Ed.* Following it, the next obvious step is **isolation**. And then, what she describes as **parasitism**, which is where *Ed* is a physical being in the story, not just an abstract concept. Turning a corner in the next chapter, Kelly takes a break to talk about a new, exciting romantic

---

[1] *Ed is a common personification of Eating Disorder, sometimes, also referred to as Ana for Anorexia. This reference will be used frequently throughout the book.*

relationship that is beginning to blossom in her life, which acts as her '**silver lining.**' Then again, the story reverts back to the central relationship in Kelly's life—*Ed*—in '***Fat Attack,***' '***Sickness,***' and '***Trapped.***' After an exhausting roller coaster of mental illness, combined with the universal struggle of growing up, Kelly turns a new page. She attempts recovery. To do this, one must have **persistence**, which means that one must betray all their disillusioned instincts and better judgment, because Lindsay, the therapist, says to. Part of recovery is letting go of secrecy and bad habits; Kelly's experience with this is addressed in '**Confession,**' where Kelly observes the secrecy all around her and within herself. In such a time in one's journey back to health, it is crucial to search for 'the good things in life,' and luckily for Kelly, she didn't have to look very far. A part two of '**Silver Lining,**' the chapter '**Love**' comes back to the boy from the beginning, and looks at their much matured, deepened relationship. '*Finally,*' the chapter entitled '**Recovery**' is when she actually starts to see results from her tireless efforts to get better. Of course, though, anorexia has one of the highest relapse rates of illnesses, and the final chapter of *Noise* is '**Recovery: Part 4,**' because it didn't work the first, second, or third time!

For Kelly, writing has served as a coping mechanism and a pursuit of art, both of which it shall continue to be. Whether writing keeps her alive or living keeps her writing, she's not entirely sure. Although through writing her first poetry novel, *Noise*, the power of words has become her religion and given her faith during a time when she lost faith in God and the community she was raised in.

A story
of coming of age and overcoming trials,
the story
of a hungry girl with a broken heart and a thousand
thoughts to swallow.

Acorn Street: Opening

When I walk down Acorn Street, I leave my driveway, my home, my millions of childhood memories, my blankey, and my parents behind, for an hour or so.

I walk past our straw-like yard and pass all of our neighbors' better yards.

I skip over the potholes, the cracks in the sidewalk, and the occasional doggie bag that either a lazy rich person or an unknowing child forgot to pick up.

I cross Maple Way, where there's a *cul de sac* and that shaggy, bronze-colored dog at the end of it, who always used to startle me as I rode around the loop, causing me to fall off my bike when my older brother Noah and I would ride that circle.

Cycle

A relentless, commonly never-ending repetition of events that persist unusually with a goal. Ex: Glycolysis.

September 22, 2016 – 4:35 P.M.

I had a fat attack[2] right before I had to leave for cheer practice. I don't know why I even had one today, though, because I actually had a pretty good day today. My therapist, Lindsay, says that fat attacks happen as a reaction to stress in other areas of my life and are then translated into panic attacks, but I wasn't even stressed today! I don't even have any tests until Monday!

Plus, the other day at cheer practice, when we practiced the pyramid formation part of our competition routine—in which I am the top of the pyramid—it was actually less scary than I thought it would be! (Not to say I didn't fall almost every time, but at least I left practice, feeling alright about it.)

Basically, what happens during a fat attack is that I look at my legs—my greatest insecurity—and my mind just implodes. I see the rest of my body normally, just as it is. Then, boom! My legs are tree trunks. In reality, I have a BMI of about 16, but that doesn't matter to my brain.

These episodes also always seem to have really good timing too…right before I have to be somewhere!

September 22, 2016 – 7:51 P.M.

WHY CAN'T I JUST EAT MY FREAKING FOOD, WEAR MY FREAKING CLOTHES, AND LIVE MY FREAKING LIFE WITHOUT FEELING LIKE A WHALE?

---

[2] "Fat attack" is a term coined by Kelly's therapist which refers to panic attacks unique to those with body dysmorphia.

September 22, 2016 – 8:05 P.M.

All I was trying to do was prepare a goddamn smoothie bowl. Yes, Pinterest, I know they're a breakfast thing but there I stood at 8:00 p.m. and this was my only chance to eat before Ed could catch up to me. Ah, but just as well, I soon found myself burning up; I could sense a layer of sweat on my face because I was afraid of exceeding 300 calories, what I had left for the day. (I like to stay under a daily total of 1,200 calories.)

I blended some frozen berries with a little almond milk, spooned it into my favorite bowl, and topped it with some oats and more berries.

Then, just as I was trying to relax myself and was about to sit down at the counter to eat, my brother Noah (who was watching T.V. in the adjacent room) began sipping from his water bottle. Immediately, my misophonia[3] kicked in: "AHHHHHHHHHHHHHH

"LA LA LA, I CAN'T HEAR IT, LA LA."

(Panting like an excited dog, forcefully plugging ears with both pointer fingers, and curling up into a ball on the kitchen floor.)

Fight-or-flight instincts awoken and sharp, I charged upstairs. But I brought the smoothie. It's the little victories, I swear.

---

[3] While often made fun of online for its seemingly relatable nature, it must be distinguished that misophonia is an actual anxiety disorder characterized by extreme discomfort and disgust triggered by irrelevant sounds such as chewing or swallowing.

September 24, 2016 – 6:53 P.M.

I probably won't let Lindsay see this one.

To be brutally honest, the main thing holding me back from suicide is that I'm afraid I will fail and end up just disabling myself or, at the very least, end up in a facility. Similar to the few other crashing and burning girls from my school. And that, of course, would only make my life ten times worse than it already is.

...That sounds so selfish, as if I have nothing to live for, but that's not it at all. I have EVERYTHING to live for. I mean, I'm a young, white schoolgirl of middle-upper class fortune. Anything I work for could just as easily by dropped right into my hands.

I don't want to say that body dysmorphia invalidates the good things in my life, but it certainly looms over everything positive in my life like a gray cloud threatening a perfect day.

And just to be clear, when I say threatening, I don't mean a wobbly cup of juice or something threatening to fall over and stain your carpet, I mean a crazy person breaking into your house and threatening you with a knife against your throat and whispering, "We can be crazy together." And you want it to stop, but the voices keep whistling in your ears, grow louder and louder until the whisper becomes a piercing scream ripping out your eardrums, and soon enough, the noise is the only thing you can hear at all. Like a glorious distraction, it echoes around your skull until you can't think clearly anymore.

Then, as my last bit of sanity trickles down the drain, the crazy person introduces himself formally for once, instead of just telling me how fat I am. The voice's name is

Ed[4]. He is an artist, and he paints pictures on mirrors and makes me fat and disproportionate. He is a lawyer and often tries to convince me that I am worthless—sometimes with a very strong case, too. He's a doctor diagnosing me as obese and a bully pounding the words into me until I actually believe it.

Next, I move away from the drain by which I lost my last wits and investigate the bathroom mirror. Finally, it hits me. I AM ED, or rather, he has embodied himself in me. I think to myself how when I was little, I never wanted to be a lawyer or a doctor or anything else that Ed is, and yet, like the best and worst of us, that is exactly what I have become. True to the child I once was, however, I do suppose I have always been a liar. Somewhere, too, in my religious-bred heart, I always knew I was capable of killing someone with the witchcraft God warns women against…I just never thought I'd be killing myself.

So tell me, reader, if you were confined not only by the debilitating physicalities of a deathly illness, but also the unrepentable guilt for bringing it onto yourself, how long would you last? How can you win? There's no gallantry in losing to a war against yourself, but there's also no pride in surrender.

---

[4] *Ed is a common personification of Eating Disorder, sometimes, also referred to as Ana for Anorexia. This reference will be used frequently throughout the book.*

Every Time

December 8, 2016

'Fat attacks' are so nauseating because I get the same feelings, thoughts, pain *'every single time.'* It's always the same thing. Same process. Same cycle. My heart breaks in the same place every time. On one hand, one would think this repetition might get boring. And yet, it is frustrating because even though it's the same old pattern *'every freaking time,'* it still gets me like it's new! It gets me every time. Every. Time.

Think about it this way: if somebody stabbed you in a specific spot once, then stabbed you there again every week, you would still always have a big-ass scab trying to heal. Even though you know they're going to stab you in that one spot next week, tell them the same thing every time, and feel the same feelings every time, so much that you're *used to it*—it's still going to bloody fucking hurt when that poor scab rips open on week 15! Even though it's the same old thing every time, it doesn't change the fact that the wound keeps healing only to be sliced open again each week. You still get that burning sensation of the skin breaking and scab being ripped away. I know that is not a relatable example at all, but it shows a physical representation of what happens to me every time I have a *'fat attack.'* The friend with the knife is *Ed,*' and the wound on your arm is '*my heart'* (and realistically, my brain as well).

And there you have it. My heart breaks in the same place every time.

Fear

July 28, 2016

I live in such fear.

Today, I am sad because my week-long religious education camp ended. A summer camp. What a nerd I am! Admittedly, I suspect that the man I'm missing in my life isn't Jesus but is a really cute blond boy from the town next door. And now I won't get to see him again. I want a boyfriend…mainly because *'I'm afraid, and tired, of being alone.'*

Also, I kind of liked getting to talk about God every day. I liked hearing the teacher's life stories, opinions, and wisdom. My family barely ever talks to each other, let alone go to or talk about feelings. I'm afraid I am but threads away from snapping the rope that connects me to God. That's the metaphor they use at camp, anyway. But if God and I are bound together by a rope, aren't I just his puppet? Is everything happening now, some kind of omen to signify I'm not actually being bound, but noosed and hung?

I'm just afraid. 'I'm afraid of not being enough'…by being 'too much.' I am afraid to take up space, in space, or on earth.

A Broken Record

Imagine what it's like to have a mind Trapped in this spinning motion,
Like a broken record player of
Constantly worrying and constantly hating and
Constantly sighing and crying and asking *Why.*

Family

Obligatory humans who bear the responsibility of raising you. A 20-year commitment at the very least. Hopefully, you got lucky.

Harvard Graduation (for Dad)

May 2014

We get back from the ceremony
And stand around you
We think
We reflect
Upon the many hours
Put into this
And yet I am sad
And happy
At the same time
That we have finished
This chapter
Of our lives.

Then Grandpa speaks
He remembers
The letter
The acceptance
An invitation to success
He knew you would
Accomplish many things.

Your high school guidance counselor said
"Don't waste your time
You're not worth it"
But you are!
You did it!
And Grandpa finished
"You graduated"

And we couldn't be prouder.
Meanwhile, I cried
Tears of joy. Of relief
I cried but for only a moment
But I did cry
For the many things
That you are
That you've done
That I've observed

I wondered at
The future, for
I could not imagine a world
Without
The light from the office
Spilling into the hallway at 1 a.m.
Without
The late nights Mom watched Hawaii 5O
Waiting for you to come home at 11 p.m.
Without
The aged bricks and reading glasses
Green ivy on the walls and
An unnecessary abundance of college sweatshirts.

But I knew a few things:
You would still be in this world of the future
And soon it would be my turn to put on the glasses.

And
If there is
One thing

That I will remember
For I can be very forgetful
Is what you
Told me
Diploma in hand
You looked me in the eyes
And asserted the words
Dreams do come true
I believe you.
In that moment
And on that day
It didn’t matter
That I was starving my way toward a slow death
That your back was still sore with stitches
Or that Grandpa’s mustache
Was actually just nose hair.
Those shouldn’t be
The things in life
That matter
Anyway.

You matter
To me.

Dad (Part One)

Alone in the car
With him
She thought to herself
How she'll *never* get this moment back
What if there's no tomorrow?
What if he doesn't live?
After all
He has…a touch…of cancer
You'll regret it whispered her mind *Say something,*
Tell him you love him
Pleaded her heart
Everything
In her wanted to reach out
To him
And yet
She kept her lips sealed tight
She felt as though
She would explode
She nearly burst at the seams
With everything she never said
But even today
She still never spoke
A word
She kept quiet
And rode softly on.

Dad (Part Two)

December 14, 2017

I don't know what it is
But you strike me
As very special.

You are a Fruit Loop in this world full of Cheerios
I just wanted to write this
To remind you
To never ever lose your color.

Because
You know, sometimes
Ugly ducklings spend their whole lives
Feeling out of place
Because
They can't swim like fish
Nor can they fly like birds
But you, oh my
You are my Trumpeter Swan.

You are my nonlinear graph
In a world hooked on conformity.

And
Although I sometimes treat you
Like an ugly duckling
Or like a candle that's been burning too long
Trust me, you are my fireworks
Trust me, I love you.

I just get
Afraid
Sometimes…
Afraid of being blinded by the colors
And it's like
The demons inside of me
Have nightmares about *melting*
Like shadows in the noon sunshine
Like witches fizzing away in a splash of water
All as I breathe in your presence.

You are so good
It's too good
To handle and that
Frightens me (and my demons)
Deeply.

My Actual Favorite Thing Ever

December 8, 2017

My actual
Favorite thing ever
Is seeing the
Little wrinkles beside your eyes
When you smile.
Nothing makes me feel
As warm and fuzzy inside
As hearing the tinkle of your laugh
And seeing those
Amazing, perfect
Little wrinkles.

Mom (Part One)

September 4, 2015

Today Grandpa came over. He started a well-intentioned conversation about my cheerleading life at school and he said he saw a picture of me on Facebook; he said he could easily pick me out of the crowd because I was the shortest. That hurt my feelings so much. I wanted to cry, but instead, I fell silent. After that, I didn't really make any effort toward conversation until he left. When they were gone, I crept up to your bedroom, where you were folding laundry.

Twisting my fingers in a knot and rocking back and forth on the balls of my feet, I mumbled: "I just wanted to tell you something that was bothering me, because Lindsay says not to bottle things up…"

"I think I know what you're going to say but you can say it if you want."

Then I started to cry. "I know, Kelly. That was a very insensitive comment for him to make—"

"It's not my fault! He doesn't know that my fucking eating disorder stunted my growth! That doesn't mean it can't change! If he's so obsessed with my height, why doesn't he notice I weigh what I did in like fifth grade? It's so unfair!"

"Shhhh. He doesn't need to know. It's not his business. You are having a slight dip in the road, but you're working hard to do everything right in order to get better."

"NOBODY UNDERSTANDS HOW HARD IT IS!" I screamed, frustrated.

And then you said precisely the right thing at the right time (for once!): "I UNDERSTAND."

Mom (Part Two)

December 2017

I remember that I didn't expect to get as sad as I did. But I did. And the next thing I knew, I was swept up in a two-hour long tornado of emotions and so, so, so many tears—two full tissue boxes to be exact.

I remember I sent you a text asking to please come to my room and bring me a granola bar because I'm lazy and you're easy. An hour later, unsurprisingly, you finally checked your phone and came up to my room.

I opened the door in my oversized tee shirt, bare legs, messy bun, hair sticking out everywhere, and only half up

And tired, bloodshot red eyes—more mascara on my cheeks than on my lashes, and I let you step into my room and thanked you for the snack.

And
You looked around
Waiting for something to happen
A little confused but still polite
And you stood there
For a second
Then turned to me and saw my red eyes
And you asked
If I was okay
That was *exactly* what I'd been waiting for
I immediately said *no* and
(Uncharacteristically)
Embraced you
And
Didn't let go
No. Nothing is okay. I am not okay. Okay?!

My sobs poured out of me
This time audible
Despite my staggered breath trying to be
Quiet
And as I moaned into your shoulder
You patted my back and
Asked me again
"What's wrong? Honey, what happened?"
But of course, that's not a simple question to answer. Not when you're me, anyway
"I don't know
I'm just so unhappy! No matter how hard I try..." And I continued to cry.

My words may seem vague
But that was the most *honest* thing I'd said
Probably all that week.

And
In your arms
I remember
It felt like I was letting my wall crash down
To reveal the stones piled up within me
And as the dust cleared
I confided in you
All my pain
In that small handful of words
"I am not okay. I am unhappy…I don't know why…"

The next ones were even heavier
"This happens every day"
"Everyday?!"
"Everyday"
"Is this what you talk to Lindsay about?"
"Yes"
"I thought you were doing better…"
"This is me being better. God, this is much better than I've been in a long time…"
And
My words hung heavy around us
But you took the weight
Like a sack of flour
And turned my worries
Into pancakes…
All with that simple hug

It seems kind of funny
For a little embrace to mean *that much* to someone
But for a human as isolated as myself
All I can say is
It was *everything*.

A Really, Really, Really Bad Day

June 8, 2017 – 4:10 p.m.

A brief rundown of my classes today, as a sophomore in high school:

History

Thousands upon thousands of Muslim refugees are currently fleeing to Europe. Borders are closing. Refugees are normal people who didn't choose to leave home; they were forced away. Aleppo and Darfur are current genocides, and I am just a bystander. The Manchester Bombing happened about a week ago.

Drama

…the entire arts program is in debt and we just found out that our teacher has been fired due to budget cuts; she won't be back next year.

English

I'm currently working on a persuasive essay about how our school's chieftain head mascot is racist and outdated. How is this still a debate in 2017?

French

A while ago, Mme. Hiver told us that Paris may be the world's symbol of romance, but France itself has pretty much given up on love and that most couples don't even get legally married anymore. Add that to the terrorist attacks, bombings, and political turmoil, and Macron really has *un gâteau en catastrophe* on his hands!

Math

I got a C on last week's test, and a B on yesterday's quiz. What's happening to me? My A is down to a B+!

Biology

A former student of Nashoba and another guy—both in their mid-20s, came to speak to my class about their decade long struggle with alcoholism and drug use. Massachusetts is the Mecca of opioid abuse right now, apparently.

The world feels like it's ending today.

Clearly, everything is in a crisis. I listed above something that went wrong or was unsettling in every single class. I also have a sore throat and a zit on my lip. Today was a tough day. The world feels like it's ending for me, at least half the time to be honest, but for one man, today, it really is.

When I walked in the door this afternoon, Dad was uncharacteristically home from work at just 2:45 p.m. Mom was gone, and Dad told me that Grandpa's high blood pressure was too much…he had an aneurysm. Mom got a call around noon, telling her to get to the hospital for goodbyes, and Grammy and all my uncles are there now too. That was literally the very first time I'd seen Dad cry in my whole (almost) 16 years of being his daughter. There were heavy tears in his red eyes. His hand was covering his face and he was apologizing for crying and I was hugging him and crying too, and we were ranting, trying to make sense of it all, coming up with our own theories about his death. Why.

My theory, which Dad agrees with, is that the heart and blood pressure problems would have been preventable if he had taken care of his body after he first started to experience the physiological difficulties of advanced aging, namely having to get a catheter. Coming from a time when males had to be ultra-masculine superheroes, this pretty much instantly took away all his dignity. Soon after, he became very depressed and eventually mute. I believe he got a false impression from the doctors that his life was over, and he was going to die. It's a hard thing to describe, but the same thing happened to me when I was anorexic I felt as though I were going to die and this only led to me giving up completely, losing weight more rapidly than I ever had before I was void of all hope

There came a point, recently, where he took the whole giving-up-on-life thing to a new extreme: *'he stopped eating and drinking.'* I KNOW RIGHT!? This is *'Grandpa Joe'* we're talking about here... He was a pretty quiet guy and all, but if there was one thing that kept him at family parties, it was food. He loved food. He ate all the time, for he was very long and thin, and his metabolism was a furnace, burning it all right up. There wasn't anything on the planet he wouldn't eat. Whenever I would come over their house as a kid, Grandpa was always sitting at the table munching away, quietly content with himself, enjoying a microwave pasta dish Grammy had warmed up for him. But then, on Easter Day of 2017, he gave all that up, which was when we all knew that things were bad...for real, this time. It was a sign.

A lady came by after a while and said that the food was ready and that it was buffet style, so Mom asked her father what he wanted to eat. He said he was fine. She asked again. He said he didn't want anything. She said, "Well, you gotta eat somethin'," and he turned away from her, shrugging her off. He wouldn't have it.

Mom told Grammy what happened, and Grammy was stunned herself. Around this time, I'd also overheard little tidbits of gossip about how he's gotten himself dehydrated multiple times, and he's fainted from it at the hospital and stuff recently. Also, that week, he had hip surgery because he was in a nursing home and somehow broke it. We don't know how. Nobody does. I suppose he's just frail; my mom read on the internet that an old person can potentially break their hip simply by standing too quickly, but, then again, he never stands up?

Over the years prior, he had grown noticeably colder as a person. At family parties, he would always just sit at the table, say nothing, and smile when Mom or Uncle Teddy would go refill his plate for him. But, over time, Mom, her brothers, and everyone started noticing that as soon as he was finished with eating, he would tell Grammy he wanted to go home. He wouldn't go for the food then stick a like he used to; he would be done with us all once he was done with his meal. This caused some tension between him and Grammy because she would always want to stay, but he would be signaling to her that he wants to leave by grabbing his coat and waiting by the door. This happened at Christmas once, and Grammy actually yelled at him because we'd just started opening presents when he wanted to leave. We'd just handed Grammy her and Grandpa's gifts, and Grammy was all "Joe, what the heck?! Don't you want to see your grandchildren open their presents?! They got you something too! We're not leaving right now ******!"

But I digress.

Now, here's a letter to Grandpa Joe, who will be in heaven in a matter of hours now, as it is 3:40 p.m. currently, and he's not supposed to make it to the morning. There's a priest down there right now doing final blessings or whatever with Mom and everyone there too.

Grandpa Joe,

You might not remember me, because we haven't talked in a long time, and I've neglected to give you so many goodbye hugs. One of the last times, I was at your house, and you'd mistaken me for the picture of seven-year-old Emilia on the calendar. But I know you. I love you. And I'm sorry for all the goodbyes I missed... The awkward moving down the chain of family see-you-laters. Auntie Paula smelling my hair, as we hug and awkwardly hugging Cousin Colin with my face in his chest. Taking a big ole kiss on the cheek from Grammy and saying 'Goodbye, I love you.' Then, casting my glance toward you in the corner, smiling politely at everyone, at me, and me wondering how much you're there and how much you even know what's going on... My conscience desperately pleading me to hug you because God knows nobody else says goodbye to you because they assume you don't want to because you don't engage in the family Conga line of goodbyes. But I know you appreciate it because every time I hugged you—like that time in the hospital and maybe a few other times at your house—you always smiled and said 'nice girl' and you've said the same thing about little Emilia. But most of the time, I didn't because I was afraid to. I do not know why, but...

I was. But I wish I had just swallowed my pride. I'm sorry for all the goodbyes I never said and all the hugs I still have reserved for you. I guess I'll have to wait a long time to give them now, instead of 'oh, I'll do it next time,' but you'll get them, I promise, because I know you're going to heaven, and I will too.

But just so you know, I never defined you by your medical bills like everybody else did, in time. When I think of you, I think of that smiling guy who played cards with Noah, Grammy, and I at the kitchen table when you babysat for us. You and Grammy got so competitive with the cards! At the time, I thought you two may actually have been arguing, but looking back, that was just the raging banter of a happy old couple.

I'd asked you to play blocks with me because Mom told me you were an engineer and would know how to make castles.

Last winter, and Mom and I came to visit. Grammy was outside, shoveling the driveway, so Mom went out to 'help,' but it just turned into a stubborn little bickering over who was going to shovel, both of them telling the other one to go inside. You and I watched from the window of the dining room, and together we laughed at them because we both knew that Mom and Grammy were—like mother like daughter—busy bees who refuse take a break, no matter how often they complain about chores. I think that might've been the only conversation I've ever had with you.

I don't really know what else to say, but that I hope this is what you wanted, and I hope you know how much all of us and Grammy and everybody loves you, and I hope you love us all back, even if you didn't say it. I think the saddest thing about your death is that so much went unsaid. It's the same way that nobody these days talks about mental health.

And now, I'm writing this letter that nobody will ever see, but at least I'll be able to read it back, say, a year from now. But your words will die with you. To be honest, you missed just as many goodbyes as me, and probably more. I can't even imagine what Mom and everyone is going through right now, but for me, someone who wasn't even super close to you, I'm crying. I'm not sad for myself though. I mean, yeah, my family will never be complete again, as you were my first loved one to pass away...and I'll have to go to my first funeral in a couple days, and the anniversary of your death will be three days before my birthday. But I'm just so sad for you. I'm sorry that this happened to you, and I'm sorry that you wanted it to. I love you Grandpa Joe.

Your granddaughter (Caroline's daughter),

Kelly

Black Dresses

June 13, 2017 – 10:57 a.m.

I walk out the doors and down the church steps. We're in rows two by two. I'm alone, in front of my parents. The sun is hot, and my silver wedges reflect the light. The church bells ring, and the organ finishes the last few chords of its song. Cars outside go by. I see a truck. For a Main Street road, they're going kind of slow, acknowledging the cluster of people in black dresses and suit jackets, walking out of the church. If I were one of them, on the outside, I would wonder what the story was, but only for a moment, then my mind would fleet on to the next thing. They don't know who we are. They didn't know Joe. And I notice how the limo is square at the back, so they can fit the casket in it, I assume. I watch Grammy get into it. Now that we're outside, I join up with Mom and Dad. Mom's face is red. She's holding Dad's arm. Her eyes are shiny. She tells him that she's going to go in the limo with her mom. I watch Uncle Robert get in the back seat of the limo. Noah, Dad, and I walk in silence to the car. Oh, the silence. A respectful silence. The cars going by may be going on with life, but for us, life has slowed down. We skipped work and school on a Tuesday to wear black dresses and listen to a priest who never even met Grandpa tell us how great he was and that he's going to heaven. And the whole time I've been telling myself to grow up, don't cry, you're now sixteen and two entire days old. And as I get into the car and take one last glimpse of the brick church in all its glory, I mentally check my first funeral off the bucket list. (Honestly, *pun intended*. I don't care anymore.)

Yellow Roses

June 13, 2017 – 2:39 p.m.

The air smells like air conditioning, stale tears, and wilting flowers.

I think back to the morning and the pretty yellow roses, and I hope Grandpa is happy. Oh, the beautiful yellow roses.

Each one represents one of your children

And they decorated your casket better than any garden. Oh, how I wish you could've seen these beautiful

Yellow roses.
Your *favorite* yellow roses.

I just wish I knew what you were thinking when you died.

I just wish I hadn't had to find out about your favorite flower this way.

I hope there are yellow roses for you in Heaven, my love. See you soon, Grandpa.

Acorn Street: Part 2: Riley's House

We met when we were just two years old at a neighbor's birthday party and have been sisters ever since. We were 'bus buddies' all the way from kindergarten to eighth grade. We shared several bus drivers, but our favorite was Bob. We used to say his name like 'Baaaahhhbb,' and he would yell back, "Are there sheep back there?"

We would get all excited because we thought he was actually serious. To be honest, sometimes, in looking back, I can't even tell. He was unpredictable. He was overweight, always wore the same medium wash blue jeans, and had hair as white as snow. Our least favorite bus driver was Nancy. She had the best intentions, but the worst social skills. The best memory I have of her was when one of the streets along our bus route was getting paved, and *'she went right through it.'* As we came upon the workers in their bright yellow shirts, I saw their angry faces, middle fingers, and heard them yelling at Nancy. She drove right through their set up, knocking down orange cones, and leaving black tar steaks the next mile down the street. Nobody messes with her bus route, that's for sure!

In second grade, when everyone was really into *Harry Potter*, my favorite characters were Ron's brothers, Fred and George. I told Riley that we needed to become pranksters, so we began brainstorming naughty things we could do. We came up with what we thought was the absolute most hilarious thing in all of 2008…We found an old lollipop stick covered in floor-of-the-bus crap, like hair and dirt. It was a Friday, though, and we would have to wait until Monday to carry out our plan, so I hid the lollipop stick behind a plant vase in my living room over the weekend. Looking back, that's pretty disgusting. But at the time, it was exhilarating. On Monday, we wrapped it up all nice in some computer paper. In those days, all the boys were completely obsessed with Bakugans, which were basically plastic balls that opened into monsters and other characters from the T.V. show. They're probably still out there. Anyway, we chose our favorite boy in the class, Linus, and addressed the gift to him. We wrote a note on the side saying that it was a Bakugan, then left it on his desk. We felt so mischievous I'm sure it was a lot more anticlimactic in reality as it felt at the time for Riley and me…Oh, and poor Linus.

In fourth grade, there was a new girl in my class named Jillian. She had shiny auburn hair and freckles to match. We grew to be close friends because we were both in the advanced reading group; we were reading *'Sarah, Plain and Tall,'* and I forgot what it was about, other than the fact that it was the plainest book I'd ever read. Eventually, Riley, Jillian, and I became an unbreakable trio of best friends. We were B.F.F.'s: I was the B, Riley was the F, Jillian was the second F, and we had necklaces to prove it. Everything was all fine and dandy until the annual Lip Sync show at our school approached in February; we chose 'Evacuate the Dance Floor,' and we had a whole dance routine worked out, except Jillian was clearly the star of it. She was in the middle for most of the dance, and she also gave herself a solo. What really crossed the line, though, was when she decided that she should have a costume unique to the matching ones, to which she had previously matched, and which Riley and I had been planning on wearing.

Unfortunately, in addition to other increasingly controlling behavior, it got to a point where I got into a fight with Jillian and ended our friendship. Riley tried to remain neutral. However, after about a week and a half of being dragged along by Jillian, as she watched me from a distance at recess and pretended I didn't exist from her desk across the English room, Riley confessed to me on the bus one day that she no longer wanted to be friends with Jillian either. It was on this day that Riley and I made a pact to never let people get between us. After all, it takes two to tango, but that three's a crowd!

In seventh grade, when I was really sick, I remember being on the playground with Riley at recess, and she asked me why I was wearing my North Face jacket zipped up to my neck and long jeans in the beginning of May. I said I was cold. She asked me if I was okay. I confided in her that I'd been diagnosed with a low heart rate of 40-something beats per minute. Her eyes were frightened, and she looked at me questioningly, as if she wanted to press me further, but I was very distant, so she did not egg me on much past that. It doesn't sound like much, but she was actually the furthest any of my friends went about questioning me; everyone else caught secretive glances at the bones sticking out from my frame right and left and didn't dare to ask why. This is why I love you, Riley.

Why Society Sucks

Unattainable standards, inequality, conformity, etc. Too many smart people being made to feel worthless, and too many not-smart people running governments and big industries.

Some Simple Advice by a 14-Year-Old

Be the person who waves
Not the one who didn’t wave back.

It Just Happens

People wonder
Why
There is so much pain
In the world
So much suffering
How could God
Let this happen?
How could
He hurt
The people he loves?

But maybe
He doesn't let it happen
He doesn't will it to

Maybe
The sky looked away
The day she fell from it

Maybe
Earth rolled its eyes
When she crashed into the dirt

Maybe
Earth's people pretended not to hear
When she pleaded for help
Clearly
Society likes to pretend
That everything is fine 100% of the time

“We’re all happy
And if you’re not happy
Then you’re not one of us.”

Maybe
God didn’t promise
Humanity
That everything would be fine
100% of the time.

Clearly
Society promised
Its consumers
That
And when it didn’t work out
They pointed fingers and said that
God looked away
When they suffered
It’s his fault.

So that girl
Who fell from the sky
Grew up
Untrusting
Cold
Alone
Because nobody cared to help her
When she trusted they would listen
So she never asked again
Because she knew they couldn’t
And she grew up cruel and unyielding.

Why do we hurt the ones we love most?

In my experience
I never will it to happen
And yet I still surprise myself
With how cruel I can be
It's unprecedented
Maybe
It just
Happens…

"Indeed,
Allah does not wrong the people at all
But it is
The people
Who are wronging
Themselves"
Quran 10:44

uman

r 4, 2016

I am so depressed these days… I am so sick of life.

I had a Catholic confirmation-meeting thing tonight at the church. It made me think that instead of getting confirmed so I can be closer to God, *why don't I just die right now and go to heaven now to meet up with him? Why do I have to endure life first? I hate life. Let's just skip the waiting and cut to the point, you know?*

I mean, of course, there are good things and wonderful things and amazing things in this world. But when I see good things happening to people, it just makes me feel worse—jealous and bitter—because they're allowed to experience joy when I can't. When good things happen to me, I immediately conclude that my flaws—like being short or fat or stupid or female—invalidate anything good that I do or anything positive that happens to me, and the good moment is drowned.

Take Christmas for example: it's the most wonderful time of the year, right? Well, some would say that. For me, when I get presents on Christmas morning, I don't get excited. I feel guilty. Guilty that everyone is wasting their hard-earned money on an ugly and broken piece of shit, with absolutely no value in this life or the next, just to be polite. This year, I've been thinking about how everyone else's houses have lights up and I haven't even decorated my room yet, and how I skipped out on our family Christmas tree decorating because I was 'too busy' with crap, like working out and sulking alone in my room Why is everyone having a good time except me? I can't even remember what happiness feels like, or when I experienced it last…

It's very hard to describe, but the way I think about myself, I'm embarrassed to do anything. It makes me feel silly when I act like a normal human being because I can't do normal human being things without looking like I'm a try-hard or merely mimicking normal human beings. Because I'm not normal. I'm not cool; I'm not hot; I'm not tall; I'm not loud; *'I'm not human.'* Maybe, my parents don't think so, and maybe my friends wouldn't say so, but at the same time, it's not that I care what *other* people think, I care about what *'I'* think. And you know what I think? *'Fuck.'*

Chocolate Rice Cereal and the Future of America

November 10, 2016, Two Days After 2016 Presidential Election

I sit at the table alone at 11:00 p.m. with my chocolate cereal
I see the little brown rice crisps
Floating around in the white almond milk.

Some are broken
Others darker with chocolate and some are lighter
Some of them stick to each other and others swim alone.

I fiddle with my spoon
And think
Will they all be okay?
With Trump now in charge of the country
Are they going to be okay?

Will the broken get the care they need?
Or will they break further?

Will the dark-colored be equal to the light-colored ones? Or will they be eaten around and left at the bottom of the bowl for the dishwasher to swallow?

Will it matter which partners they prefer, who they like to stick to? Or will they be shamed for the way their sugar coating has made them and led them to bind to that other one?

Will this cereal be chewed up and spat out
Like a poor woman on the New York
City streets?

What will become of this world? I worry about what cereal will be like five years from now.

Heck, what about the humans?

Will the suffering, the needy, the elderly, the black, the white the male, the female, the in-between, the gay, the straight AND the chocolate brown rice crisps all be okay?!

Acorn Street: Part 3: The Reporter's House

Soon after Julianne's house (you'll read about her later) is 'The Reporter's House.' He is a reporter on *Fox News* or something fancy. I don't know much about him, but I remember that the one time I actually watched him on T.V. was when he interviewed runners in the Boston Marathon in the year 2010 or something. (I don't watch T.V. much.) I'm sure that on a normal day, he's a great reporter, but I remember laughing so hard and telling my mom about it at least four times while watching that day because it was a boiling 90 degrees outside, and he was wearing a black shirt, so you can imagine how it went. He jogged desperately from person to person, trying to keep up with the runners, dripping sweat and somehow managing to make his black shirt even darker around his armpits. Whenever he reached someone who wanted to talk, he would breathily spit at them the same question he'd asked the past three runners, and they would respond with a brief and uninformative answer because they were conserving their breath for running. This went for at least an hour. Poor guy.

Anyway, he also has a son living with him who looks old enough to be out of college. His son mows the lawn for him literally '*everyday,*' and I can't stand it. To be fair, about half of the street gets their lawns mowed every single day, which irks me even more. When you're rich, I guess you can throw money away on a bunch of Mexican men, listening to Britney Spears while painting your roof or reseeding your lawn.

My family has 'never' ever hired someone to do our lawn for us. Granted, that's why we have literally the worst lawn—like actual straw—on the street during the hot summer months, but I still feel oddly dignified by our yellow lawn…like maybe we're *'more human'* than the expensive roll out grass people, you know?

Not Enough

June 21, 2017

I'm **not** social **enough**. I never invite friends to places, and whenever I'm invited somewhere else, I'm super awkward and **not** fun **enough**. I'm not outgoing enough, and I'm never the life of the party. *'I am a mute smile of a teenage girl.'* I sit there at the party or whatever it is for four hours straight, and smile and nod. The same thing goes for family parties. I'm **never** talkative **enough** because I've given up on opening my mouth to speak because every time I do, I get interrupted or talked over. They say it's because I'm **not** loud **enough,** but really, I think it's because I'm just **not** interesting **enough**.

I'm **never** around **enough**. Whenever my boyfriend wants to hang out, I always make him leave early because I need to be alone. Not because I don't love him enough to want him to stay, but because I'm **not** prepared **enough** for tomorrow. I'm not smart enough to ace my tests without studying, and my GPA is **never** high **enough,** so I have to study even if I know everything. I'll never get into Harvard anyway, though, because I'm **not** scholarly **enough,** and I'm not extraordinary enough, and I'm **not** involved **enough** in extracurricular activities, but I literally don't have time **enough** for anything else because I'm **not** good **enough** at time management. I'm **not** good **enough**. Aidan is so good at compliments. It pains me that I'm **never** clever **enough** to come up with cute things to say back to him because I'm **not** smooth **enough,** and I'm **not** creative **enough,** and I'm **not** straight-up **enough** to tell him how much I love his hair and how I love it when he picks me up, and how I love hearing him say my name. I do this to Mom, Dad, and my brother too. I'm **never** bold **enough** to say how much I appreciate them in my life. I'm **not** thankful **enough**. I don't speak my heart **enough**. *'I am **not enough**.'*

Acorn Street: Part 4: The Mustard Green House

A few houses over from mine is a million-dollar house with a nice porch, a tree house in the back, and a large window above the three-car garage. A family of four lived here—the parents and two gorgeous daughters with straight brown hair and freckles across their noses. Much older than me, the two girls were in seventh or eighth grade when I was in first grade. I remember because they used to always say 'hi' to me in the too narrow hallways of our brick K-8 school building, saying I was adorable, and that we were friends. I genuinely considered them my best friends for a while, and I thought about them a lot. But we never hung out or anything, obviously. Also, I'd never met their parents, although I was glad I hadn't, because Mom always ranted about them, and not in a good way. Every Halloween, she would tell us to steal extra candy from their basket because they always pretended to not be home when my older brother Noah would try to sell popcorn to them for Boy Scouts.

As for the house itself, I had always found it a nuisance to our street because they re-painted it a new color every year, it seemed. First, it was a gross mustard yellow, and then for a time, it was bread mold green, and then it switched back and forth between those two colors for a good set of years—*as if* it would help! At that point, you might as well just mix them together! It's not getting any prettier, honey.

I had always wondered if the people inside changed color as often as the outside did…

To Women

You are more beautiful than you will ever know, and more intelligent and powerful than you have ever been treated.

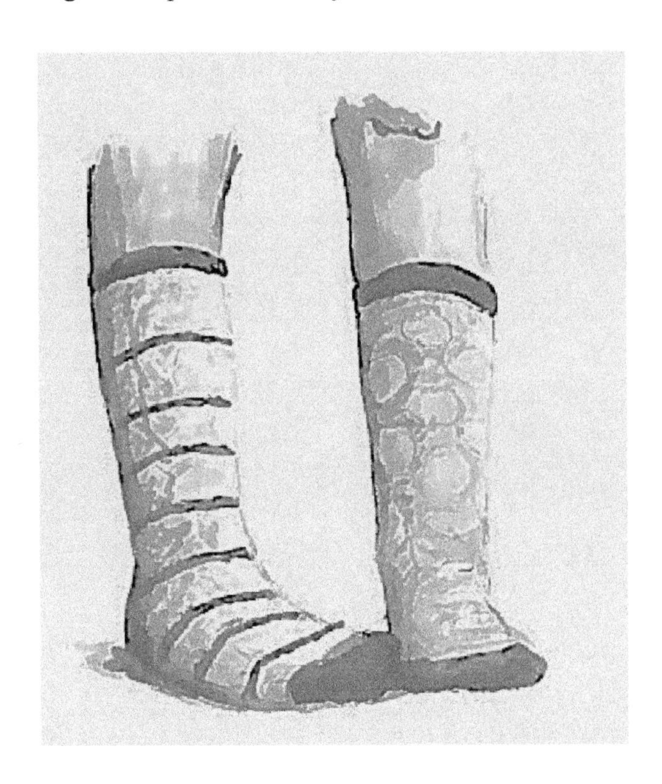

The Other Part of Me

April 14, 2017

Part of me says that I don't fit in with my friends, that I am unpopular, that I am an embarrassment, and that nobody really likes me. But the other part of me dares to be social. *So, I socialize.*

Part of me says I am a curse to that beautiful boy, for I don't know how he ever fell for me, and that I am ugly and not worthy of affection. But the other part of me dares to love. *So, I love.*

Part of me says that my family wishes they weren't tied down by me, that I am a mistake, and unworthy of their time. But the other part of me dares to accept the love I am given. *So, I accept the love I am given.*

Part of me says that I am disgrace to humanity, that I am fat and ugly, short and insignificant, and unworthy of taking up space on this earth. But the other part of me dares to feed myself. *So, I eat.*

Part of me says that I'll never be a winner, I'll never be fast enough to catch my dreams. That I'm a joke to everyone who watches the fat on my legs jiggle as I run. But the other part of me dares to run. *So, I run.*

Part of me says that I do not deserve the very ground I walk on, I do not deserve heaven nor hell, and the life I lead is unworthy of living. But God dares me to live. *So, I live.*

Part of me says many things, but I dare to listen to the *other*. It is okay to be *other*. Please, dare to be *other*.

"We Accept the Love We Think We Deserve"[5]

September 14, 2017 – 7:50 p.m.

Have you ever seen *The Perks of Being a Wallflower*? It's a movie from 2012 about a socially awkward freshman named Charlie who befriends two counterculture seniors who help him uncover a pent-up mental illness. One of the most quoted scenes from the movie is one where Charlie and the unconventionally beautiful Sam address a sexual tension between them. Charlie asks her why she gives herself up to guys so easily and she explains that she has very little self-worth and doesn't believe she is worthy of meaningful affection. Then comes my absolute favorite line, which takes to heart everything I'm about to rant about: **"we accept the love we think we deserve."**

Okay, so, this entire thought dawned on me the other day when how my friend Gracey told me today that the adorable Mei Huang is dating GARRETT WILSON: overweight since like third grade, unintelligent and failing CP Chemistry, awfully rude, and—my personal favorite—spends his summers running a fucking ketchup stand outside our old middle school.

"OMG, why would she choose him?! Like, literally, he's fat and a jerk!"

"I know, right! Ugh, *she just wants attention!*"

But wait. Mei isn't stupid. We accept the love we think we deserve. The pairing may seem like a stark downgrade

[5] Quote from the movie *The Perks of Being a Wallflower*.

for Gracey and I looking on, but Mie wouldn't be dating him if she knew she was better than him in literally every way. And knowing them both, it makes me sad that she must not think she can do better.

And then I thought about myself—being of similar stature despite the racial difference. My boyfriend is wonderfully handsome and kind, so I'm not lacking there, but what about the fact that I'm literally slowly dying of starvation as I write this? When I had once been somewhat close with Mie, I recall being very jealous of her nonchalance, once complaining about the size of her thighs while at the same time eating a big, chocolatey brownie, hundreds of calories worth. She'd have given anything to be as skinny as me, I'm the one who actually gave it all up…you know, food and everything… I should be one to talk, being so hypocritical as to judge Mie for Garrett when I punish myself the same way with food. In fact, Aidan and I have been discussing the subject for some time now, and he's made me realize my unexpected popularity at school isn't for the reason I'd intrinsically thought.

"Because I dress really cute and never eat dinner, right?"

"Kelly, listen to yourself! You're in all AP classes, you're always nice to everyone, and you wrote a book; you think people don't give a shit about that stuff, but take the time to judge what you're wearing? Take it from a guy: they don't."

I guess I'd never really given much thought to Aidan's perspective on it all, and how very *heartbreaking* it must be for him to have to witness a person who is a beautiful girl in his eyes genuinely believe she is *worthless* enough to hurt herself. No use in speculating; he told me that himself.

Do you realize just how ingrained an idea must be in someone's head to form it into a habit? Do you have any idea how many times a day I think about weight and food?! How many calculations I make in my head?! I'll give you a hint: it's hundreds of powers higher than just three times a day.

And here, my swimming anxieties formulated into one cohesive conclusion: SOCIETY IS SO FUCKED UP! I always thought it was just a flaw in *'me'*—that anorexia caused me to hyper-focus on the superficial, which, maybe it did, in part, but who knows? Maybe, I would never have even developed anorexia if I hadn't been brought up in a culture that obsesses over appearances. I mean, until now, it always sounded really cliché to me when adults said that kind of stuff—you know, the old "it's on the inside that counts" and shit like that which isn't even helpful at all but always makes adults feel clever. I cannot believe I only now noticed how fucked up today's society really is, especially in the media, for teaching our daughters to base their self-worth off beauty and—maybe even worse—for teaching our sons to perpetuate this cycle. So how dare you, society. How dare you and fuck you! For tricking fifteen-year-olds like me into valuing the superficial affection and catcalls we never even asked for over genuine connection. And, most importantly, for hiding from us the dangerously splendid truth, which is that *we deserve better.*

Gravity

December 24, 2017

To the senior boy who camps out at my locker to hit on me in between classes:

I could defy
Gravity
With how hard
I'm
NOT
Falling for you
Fly away, little birdie
Shoo, shoo.

The Best Compliment I've Ever Received

September 27, 2017

"You are truly ***remarkable***. You are such a *wonderful* person.
But not the same way that everyone else is wonderful. You're *different* and you're *special*. You're so *wonderful*, Kelly, and I need, need, need you to see it.
(tears)
Oh gosh, ha-ha, you can see I'm getting emotional now. It's just that I grew up very close to where you live, and I don't know, I can relate…you remind me of myself. I care a lot about you, Kelly."

A Message for My Future Daughter

December 4, 2017

Please don't ever let life get you down
My love
The best advice I can give you
From my very few years of experience thus far, is to
Wear bright lipstick
Dance in the rain
Eat cake for breakfast
Laugh so much that you cry
And
Never never ever ever ever let boys be mean to you.

Society's Definition of Beauty

1. Clear, clean, and fair skin
2. Soft hands with painted nails
3. Big, beautiful blue eyes and long lashes
4. Makeup, and lots of it
5. Straight white teeth
6. Long, shiny blonde hair in soft curls
7. Perfectly sculpted body
8. The latest Abercrombie clothes (and, of course, the body to fit into them)
9. A little too much sweet, fruity perfume
10. Long, thin, silky, and sexy shaved legs

So…basically, be a Barbie Doll.

Because that's all you are to society anyway: a doll. A puppet with strings attached to each of these 1 2 3 4 5 6 7 8 9 10 items.

My advice: *'snip your strings and cut yourself loose.'* May you be please be '*human.*'

If you must choose between the two, please, please choose *'human'* over *'beautiful.'* Please learn from my mistake.

The Actual Definition of Beauty:

[Insert your name here]

Love Myself

Let me tell you a secret:
There is a part of me
That wants to love myself:
My mascara stained cheeks
My freckles
And the scar on my knee
The way my blue eyes glow
Like electricity
When I cry
I wish I could love the fat on my thighs
My collarbones
And my wavy hair
I could love my stretch marks
My clear frame glasses
And my C in AP Chemistry…

What if I loved my body
So much
That I never skipped meals?
What if I never overdosed?
Never isolated myself
And never
Let myself believe
I was worthless?

I wonder what I'd
Be doing now
Had a never started a diet

At 12 years old
I wonder how close
I'd be with my dad
If I hadn't scarred his heart
Forever
I wonder how many
Friends
I'd have now
If I hadn't pushed them all
Away.

And although
The past has passed
Someday
I wish to love myself
So much
That I would
Never
Ever
Put *Ed* before
Myself.

Conformity

October 10, 2017 – 5:33 p.m.

Because you know what, my darling
Beauty changes
Why listen to what pop culture says is *perfection*
When it's bound to change
By the time you're out of college?

My history teacher Mr. Coleman
Said that some 40% of my generation
Once all grown up
Are predicted to hold jobs that haven't even been invented yet.

And
I bet in the year 1969 they
Never
Thought that *glitter eyebrows* would be on the runway…
But welcome to 2017 everyone.

My point is
That my goal
In life
From now on
Is to be *neon socks* or *glitter green eyebrows* or *whipped cream on bacon* or *beetroot muffins*
Not because the world says that it's fashionable
But because that's who I am and
It'll be fashionable when I make it fashionable.

Perfect

December 11, 2017

The funny thing
Is that
One cannot become a perfect human
Ever.

Immediately
You focused on the word "perfect"
"*But there's no such thing as perfect*!"
Shut the hell up.

Nobody can use
Anorexia
As a means of becoming
The perfect human
Because
Anorexia
Takes away
Your *humanity*
Your feelings
Your body
Your cognitive nerve functioning
Your sleep…
I mean really
What is even left of you?

A carcass of who you once were
I say this from experience.

It is much wiser
To try to be *human*
Before trying to be *perfect*
They must live separate
And
You'll achieve one much quicker than
The other.

Self-Love

October 10, 2017

I've never wanted anything more in my whole life than to know that the world loved me the same way I wandered at it passionately with sparkling eyes as a little girl.

That's what I wanted when I took my best things to Show and Tell: *attention, to know that people thought I was cool enough to be their friend.*

That's what I wanted when I wore that tight skirt to impress the guy I liked: *validation, to know I was good enough for you.*

That's what I wanted when I said I would leave and never come back: *a hug; to know you needed me.*

This is what I want someday:
To be so self-sufficient and love myself enough
That I don't need validation from the rest of the world.
Maybe this whole time, in all these 16 years of mine,
I've been telling myself
That I'm working toward a better me,
But in reality,
I was chasing *society's validation, not my own.*

I hope someday—
Maybe as a New Year's resolution—
To *stop* chasing the world and *start* chasing myself.
All this time I've been joining clubs I don't want to be part of and
Being polite to people I hate and
Taking classes that I don't care about and

Hating on myself because
The whole time, I didn't think I was good enough. *Starving myself*
Because *I wasn't enough but I was still too much*
Too much *space* (Maybe a *waste* of space)
Maybe I would allow myself to take up more physical space and
Stop starving myself if
I felt like I was worthy as a person and
Worthy of taking up space.

I kind of think it's the way I was brought up—
In a middle-upper class white society
Fabricated by half-priced diamonds and loose dollar bills
But how can environment be at the same time responsible
For my good manners, respectable education, and yet
Simultaneously for my hyper-superficial habits?

Maybe it's just conformity's fault
I feel like I should start thinking more for myself.

Instead of viewing myself through the lenses of Worldly Idealism.

Freezing

The hardening of a human shell, and the buildup of masks and lies; the pretext for isolation. Generally, a series of events or thoughts which may bring one to a conclusion that they must run and hide. It tends to be the last straw for a person when they've tried being vulnerable and got rejected every time.

Acorn Street: Part 5: The Ross House

Around the bend of the street coming from my lot, I pass the Ross House—the big happy family of two rock star parents, seven smiling, bouncy children, and three fluffy dogs.

I remember how Julianne always wanted to be my friend, ever since we were little. According to Mom, she'd wanted a play date with me since we were only four years old. But I never wanted to socialize, until, finally at some point during elementary school we *did* have a playdate.

I went over her house, and we played with cardboard boxes. We stole candy out of a stash in the butler's pantry, and she also showed me her newest puppy, a little pug named Savannah. She then showed me her older sister Harper's room, which had a green and blue spotted carpet on the floor and horse posters all over the walls. I thought it was the best thing since sliced bread, since I had always secretly looked up to Harper because she was extremely pretty. She had light brown hair that fell in soft waves over her shoulders, striking green eyes, and adorable freckles. Not to mention, her outfits were so put-together, I swear, they were taken straight from my dream closet. I'd never talked to Harper before, though.

Eventually, we decided to go outside and get some sunshine in the backyard. There, Mrs. Ross was babysitting the little redhead kids from a couple houses over along the *cul de sac*, who had that copper-colored dog that always chased my brother and I when we rode our bikes around the circle. They were playing on the zip line in their backyard.

Julianne and I played in the dirt; we'd begun to dig a hole by a tree when we came upon an old rusty wrench. We jumped up, excited, and ran over screaming to Mr. and Mrs. Ross of our finding, and thought that *maybe the people who had lived in their house before them, like Native Americans, had left it there!* (At that age, Native Americans and past house owners were the same thing…The same way peanut butter was the glue that held the days together, and the way one could feel completely fulfilled in life just from blowing the most perfect, largest bubble.)

Later, in middle school, I remember how Julianne was one of the *popular* girls, with her straight blond hair, blue eyes, perfect butt, and long legs. I desperately wanted to be part of her friend group because I had a massive crush on one of the popular boys.

His name was Jared, and I was as in love, as a sixth grader could be, with his long black eyelashes, Greek skin, chocolate brown eyes, and outgoing personality. One day, in the fall of sixth grade, one of the popular girls wasn't on the bus, so I slid into her seat: one of the four designated seats that everybody knew was reserved exclusively for populars. Usually, Julianne and the girl who was absent named Emma sat in that particular seat. Shannon stared at me from across the aisle, absolutely disgusted. She had the same sort of deceitful brown eyes that Jared had, and they screamed at me through her glare, asking me who I thought I was and how I could sit in that seat when I knew it was for her friends. When it was Julianne's stop, she got on the bus, and she left her friends dumbfounded: she saw me in her seat and didn't bat an eye. She said, "Hey, Kelly! Whooo! Join the party! What's up?"

My voice shook like a willow tree in embarrassingly high winds as I replied, “Oh, hey! Yeah, ha-ha, I just sat here. I didn’t realize that my seat is the one in front of us ha-ha. Oh, well…I like your sweatshirt, ha-ha…”

All said and done, although Julianne and I grew to be good friends, her efforts to adopt me into the friend group never worked out. Shannon’s eyes continued to glare at me, and my entire existence to the popular group was shattered, swept up, and quickly forgotten when Jared found out I liked him.

Looking back, I should never have cared about popularity; if I hadn’t, it would’ve saved me a whole lot of time, money, friends, and tears. But I—like most middle-schoolers somewhere deep in my complex sixth grade social life—got lost in the trap of conformity.

And I lost my best friend, my crush, my dignity, and my mind because of it.

Adam

May 30, 2016

I told myself that, even when I knew in my heart that I only liked you as a friend, I wanted to open my heart to as much love as I could take in, so *I won't exclude*—for I had gone so many years, blocking everything out from my parents to the stars. And I really just wanted *to love something again.* I didn't mean to force anything, but, like I said, I had not been able to use my heart for about three years, then suddenly…*I could.* I don't know if my heart is 100%, but it's 90% at least? At least, I hope.

(What an exhilarating, yet so rare and unrelatable feeling it is, to physically not be able to think or feel. Then, you get your senses back, and you feel like you just want to run at life, go smell every candle in Yankee Candle even if the sales guy is stressed out because you haven't bought anything. Wrap Dad in a big hug because you haven't been within ten feet of him for three years; let him pick you up and swing you around like he did when you were a little girl; taste exotic fruits because you can finally eat; sing for hours until your throat is raspy and sore because you love to sing and you haven't been able to connect to music in so long because your brain didn't care…)

And after all the awkwardness I caused, *'you said no.'* Why did you compliment me all the time and voluntarily sit next to me in the front row of Freshman World History and choose me for partners and call me up late at night for essay help and talk for hours about your family and school and purpose in life? Why did you bother with me if you weren't into me? … I'm definitely not giving you my homework ever again. Never again.

Acorn Street: Part 6: Sweat and Tears

It was the street on which I sprinted my heart out, for about a mile or so, after my first appointment with my therapist Lindsay. I was absolutely boiling with frustration, with steam coming out of my ears and tears running down my cheeks, as I tore down the street in my daytime clothes, not even caring how crazy I looked. And how my brother's hot friend Sean waved and said 'hey' to me from his yard (where he was playing with his lacrosse stuff) on my way back. I waved and said, "Hi," wiped some tears and sweat from my face as I turned away, so embarrassed that I ran home even faster.

I Want a Boyfriend, Don't We All???

December 2, 2016

I want a boyfriend…not because I *'need'* one, or because I need someone telling me I'm pretty all the time, or because I want someone to open doors for me, or because I'm starving for my first kiss. I want one because I'm at the point in my life now where I can love myself (enough) to be able to afford to love another human being too.

Granted, I have ups and downs, but I'm further along than I've ever been with my mental health, and I know I'm ready because that kind of intimate love is something I starve for. Whereas in the past, I was too sick and numb to feel any sexual attraction at all. It was physically impossible because the neurotransmitters in my brain didn't click anymore because there wasn't any food to provide the energy for that to happen. I know it's a symptom of anorexia because I remember the doctors used to ask me if I could feel anything…any attraction, excitement, emotion, passion…I couldn't.

After I gained back my weight in the eighth grade, I had a few crushes in school, but nothing noteworthy more so than health at this point, I think it's the age. I have theorized that there comes a point in life when the love from your family and friends just isn't enough to fill your affectional needs. Like physical needs, like food or oxygen. Humans have a psychological need for love; we talked about it in English once. I think that once people reach a certain age or maturity level, not only do they require the love from their family and friends, but also another category which emerges somewhere in the teenage years for most people—an intimate romantic love. It's the same way that affection from your parents is enough as a small child, but around the age that children usually start kindergarten, they start craving the attention of their classmates and seeking friendships.

Another reason—an admittedly shallower reason—why I really want a boyfriend right now is that *'everyone else has one.'* I mean, yeah, that sounds really bad. But hear me out: by being a 'Single Pringle' as a sophomore in high school, not only am I missing out on the stuff that all my friends get to do with their partners (like text their boyfriends and kiss them and go on dates), but I also miss out on activities *'with my friends'* (like double dates or boy-girl parties, for example).

I mean, think about it…I'm always, *'always,'* always third wheeling with someone. There are couples everywhere. Usually, I third wheel Noelle and her boyfriend because Noelle is my best friend even though I know I'm not *'her'* best friend because she said that *'he'* is her best friend. The three of us are even a lab group in F period Honors Biology…cringy, I know. They try to make me feel better by saying that her boyfriend is the one who's third wheeling her and I—which gets a chuckle out of me—but it doesn't actually help that much.

Take tonight for example too; it was Natasha's sweet sixteenth at the Celebration Inn Hotel. I sat at our table *'smack'* in between two couples—one of which was Noelle and her boyfriend. Both couples were on each other in one way or another. Meanwhile, the only other kids from my school at the party were Karmin Jacobs (hot popular guy), Josh Gillis (average nice guy), and Alexa Willow…Alexa was dressed completely inappropriately. She might as well not have even worn a skirt at all, because hers was even shorter than the spandex I had on underneath my dress! The boys acknowledged that she looked like a *'prostitute'* and that Josh 'might have to pay her at the end of the night.' Granted, I was told she'd just been dumped by *her* boyfriend, and was seemingly trying to compensate herself…still, the attention she received only magnified my own unattractiveness.

Meanwhile, I was alone, alone, alone, alone, so, so, so *'single.'* I sat there the whole night and didn't have any fun until another one of my girlfriends from school showed up with 30 minutes left in the night. We danced, which is actually very uncharacteristic for me, but I can't deny the broad smile on my face as we swayed to the beat of Five Seconds of Summer's *'Heartbreak Girl.'* I was eyeing Karmin most of the time, though, to see if they'd notice my maroon dress fluttering in the flashing lights and my heels lightly tapping the floor. I felt like I was in a music video, but I needed a male counterpart to play the love interest.

Diamonds

I think
My face
Is melting
Whenever this happens
My eyes turn to glass
Then they melt
Like hot metal
Or wax
The shards of glass run down my cheeks
But don't tear my porcelain face
They speckle the ground
Like it's raining diamonds
And
I stand there with my feet
Looking back at me
Reminding me of how sad I am.
And against the tar earth
The diamonds are stars on a black sky
And I—
I am standing on it
Why, oh, why
Do I stomp on everything beautiful?
I do not wish to *mess it up*
But my feet crunch away
As I walk over to you
And the diamonds are
Turned to salt.

The Grieving

My heart shattered like broken glass
On concrete reality
That cold December night
As crisp as a ripe green apple
And dark like a troubled mind
When the moon
Was so thin
It dared to disappear altogether
Just as he had.

And the stars looked away
Because they couldn't handle my tears
Like that feeling
When a beautiful person
Is broken
And you just well up inside
Like you're so, so sorry the world did this
To them.

Isolation

The intentional act of secluding oneself from the rest of society, often used as a coping mechanism for depression, anxiety, or other emotional conditions and circumstances. Alone with only themselves and their thoughts, one may have one friend, their thoughts, or none. In either case, they're screwed.

Shame

November 30, 2016

'Don't feel shame, don't feel shame, don't feel shame.'

That's what Lindsay tells me. *'But I do.'* I can't help it. I feel like a Jell-O sack of fat, and I feel *'shame.'* I feel *'gross.'* I feel *'embarrassed,'* like I don't want anyone to see me. I am *'ashamed,'* apologetic for the way that I am, and *'angry'* that it has to be this way… *'angry'* that I'm stuck in this body, in this life, under these circumstances. And tears form a salty stream dripping down my squinting face because I pity myself. I *'am'* rock bottom. I am coal in a stocking. I am the last crumbs at the bottom of the chip bag that nobody wants to eat. *'I want to die.'* I want to escape. ***'I want to stop feeling feelings that tear me apart.'***

The optimism in me says *"But what about all the good things and good memories you gave people?"* I'm sure that's true…But on nights like this, I think that I don't *'want'* to be in any more memories; I don't *'want'* to be seen; I don't *'want'* anyone to know me, to see me, to know who I am, and associate me with the image of me that's fat. I don't *'want'* people to know the fat me that I know. *'I don't want people to know the fat me.'*

Unworthy

You are a curse to that beautiful boy
Who rearranges the stars in the sky
Like pieces of a puzzle
He scrambles all the letters
And makes them write your name
He shouts to the Heavens
Proclaiming his love for you.

And yet
You do not hear him.

The Wanting

Loose lips sink ships
But quiet hearts burn cities.

Last Night

June 1, 2017

Its realizing that you've hurt him…you are a curse to that beautiful boy, and by God, you don't deserve him.

He deserves the entire world and all the stars, and even then, it might not be enough to show him how much you love him. It's all the guilt of his tears, crashing down on you like stormy waves, and the darkness of your room becomes the black of night strobed by lightning, and you just think to yourself about how you were so angry—and you still are—about how he wronged you…

And yet, I could drown oceans with what I feel for him.

Gosh, I love him. He is what I think about every night to put myself to sleep…But because we are now fighting, and he's mad at me, and I was mean to him, I feel like I can't think about him…So now, I have nothing to think about to put me to sleep. Sure, there are plenty of good things in my life, like family, birthdays, spring, movies, and friends. But none of them matter without him. *'They're* not dream worthy. Only *'him.'*

Moral of the story is that now I can't sleep because *'there aren't any dreams to be dreamt without him in them,'* and I'm lying in bed, having a full on anxiety attack, and my head hurts, my thoughts are racing at a hundred miles an hour, and I just keep repeating, "It's gonna be okay. It's gonna be okay. It's gonna be okay. It's gonna be okay. It's gonna be okay. It's gonna be okay. It's gonna be okay." But it's not, it's not okay. He's not here and even if he was, it would be super awkward. I can't picture him, holding me tight and comforting me like I usually do when I'm upset about something because it's me who should be comforting him because it's my fault and I don't even know anymore and I repeat, "OMG what's happening right now? OMG what's happening right now? OMG what's happening right now? OMG what's happening right now? OMG what's happening right now? OMG what's happening right now?" And I'm like, "Kelly, shhhhhhhhhh. Stop it. It's gonna be okay. It's gonna be okay. It's gonna be okay. It's gonna be okay. It's gonna be okay. It's gonna be okay. It's gonna be okay." But '*I don't know.*'

And my body is glued to my bed like when you're in a roller coaster and gravity pulls you into the seat. Every muscle in my body is tense, and I'm grasping onto the comforter for dear life, and it's pulled up all the way to my neck and blankey is on my right and Teddy is on my left and I just keep asking them, "OMG what's happening right now? OMG what's happening right now? OMG what's happening right now. OMG what's happening right now? OMG what's happening right now? OMG what's happening right now?" And my head really hurts, and I keep crying, and I keep catching myself sobbing too loudly, then holding my breath, trying to be quiet because I don't want Noah or Mom or Dad or people to hear me.

And I really wish I was a turtle who could just crawl inside its shell forever because I'm so deathly afraid of hurting people. It's like *'don't touch me, get away from me, stay away, don't touch me, I DON'T WANT TO HURT YOU. AHHH! GET AWAY!'*

And I'm curled up tightly into a ball just wishing I could disappear and thinking how Aidan deserves so much better.

Eventually, I text him again because I just can't wait another seven hours for morning to get any kind of closure. So I text him, but of course, he doesn't see it because he's already gone to bed, so I continue on with my panic until, eventually, a vessel in my brain snaps from lack of oxygen or a surplus of adrenaline and I completely black out I spend the night in an eight hour panic-induced coma and claim a peaceful night's sleep in the morning

Naked

November 24, 2017

"Please help me"
I whispered
I prayed to God
(And I don't even believe in God)
"God, please help me."

I lay on my bed
In fetal position
With my mascara-stained cheeks
Pressing against my teddy bear
And my blankey
From when I was little
And I'm burning inside
I'm drying up
Like a beached fish
In the blazing sun.

I am
A rock weathering by the day
Bit by bit, being broken into
Pebbles and sand and dust
On these days
I feel so fragile and empty
That I could get
Blown away in the wind
As does the sand.

In these moments

I feel like a poor little hermit crab
Without his shell
Alone and exposed
Naked and vulnerable
And
I feel so unsafe
In my own bedroom
I wonder
How I can ever leave.

And the little world around me
Which I have known all these 16 years of mine
Often appears unfamiliar with the
Flick of a switch in my brain
As if someone has turned out the lights
On me.

Hence why I lay here:
Burning up
Drying out
Shivering like a baby
And
Crying like one, too.

On Edge

November 14, 2017

On days like this
I can't help but to hide inside myself like a turtle in its shell
Like a caged animal burrowing in the corner, shying away
From the light and the strange white faces urging it on.
I feel on edge, like a brick in my stomach I can't cough up
Like the way a cat's fur stands on its ends when threatened
I feel like I'm swaying back and forth
Wishing I could just stand still and get a grip for a minute
But my toes are peaking over the edge of a cliff
I feel that feeling
Of just being so on edge
On days like this.

Parasitism

Refers to a non-mutual relationship, where the parasite benefits at the expense of its host. Example: ticks. Figurative example: Ed.

A lot of people are undereducated about mental health because nobody talks about it. For one thing, you should know that it is not a choice. There are a lot of assumptions that anorexics are white girls and models trying to get attention and conform to societal beauty ideals. I promise you that's not it at all. Anorexia and all mental illnesses are genuine diseases and are as detrimental as any physical sickness. They are parasites of the brain.

Voices

Voice 1: You're just a kid, relax. There's no point in holding yourself to standards that raise every time you meet them.

Voice 2: You told yourself you would be happy once you reached 80lbs. You're 69 now and are just as unhappy as you were at 90. When does it stop? Will you ever be happy?

Voice 3: I don't know when I'll be happy or if I ever will be—

Voice 4: Of course you won't, you fat piece of shit. Not looking like that.

Voice 1: How could you have known *what* you wanted at first? You were so young. A few months older now and—

Voice 4: You know *now* that 80lbs is still too heavy. Damn, you had no idea how fucking fat you even *were* at 90lbs!

Voice 3: If you're unhappy with yourself now—

Voice 4: Then imagine how horrific you'd feel if you gained back weight!

Voice 2: Wait then why didn't you feel this bad at the original 90bs?

Voice 1: You should just gain back the weight you lost and go back to being a normal, healthy girl. Remember your friends—

Voice 4: What, the ones who are all prettier than you?

Voice 3: You mean the friends you used to have…

Voice 1: I'm just saying that maybe she'd actually be happier if she was healthy!

Voice 4: Yeah, shithead, cause that's why *we're* here in the first place. Do you really fucking think—

Voice 3: She can just be normal?

Voice 4: If she was normal, she wouldn't have needed *us*.

Voice 3: That's not what I meant—

Voice 1: Guys! You are yelling too loud, look at her. She's trying to take a chemistry test. Can't we all just argue about this later?

Voice 2: Oh my god, don't even say the word "later." *Snack time* is later! I haven't even stopped thinking about that apple she had for lunch! My glucose levels are so low I feel like I could just pass out—

Voice 4: Why would she eat between lunch *and* dinner? If she doesn't eat a snack, she can have something more substantial than a fucking apple for lunch.

Voice 2: Well, if she suffered through the entire school day on just 60 calories—

Voice 4: Then you can't come in here and fucking ruin all her progress with a god damn, greedy little "snack!"

Voice 1: If she worked hard for it, don't you think she deserves it?

Voice 3: It's not that she doesn't deserve it, but she's doing her future self a favor by saving the calories for another time.

Voice 1: Maybe we could treat her tomorrow with a 150-calorie breakfast instead of a 120 one? Or a clementine to go with the apple at lunch, you know, something special!

Voice 2: And the irony of that is we all know tomorrow won't go that way. Today is yesterday's tomorrow, and where's the food?

Voice 4: Off her thighs! For God fucking sake, just let her starve! That's why we're here! It's what she wants!

Voice 1: But—

Voice 2: It's what she wants?

Voice 3: I guess it is, technically, what she says she wants.

Voice 4: It’s what we all want!

Voice 5: Yes, it’s what I want.

Flashbacks

Does anyone else
Have those moments
Where everything is fine
You're happy
You're moving on in life

But then at the most
Random times
Like at the
Grocery store
School
Or the
Gym

Everything goes dark
Like someone turned a switch
In your brain
And you're back where you were
Three years ago

And the memories

Of suffering
Of pain
Of lies
Of betrayal

All come rushing back into you

As if someone
Is playing the memories on a film
And forcing your eyelids open
And he's strapped you to your chair
So all you can do
Just sit there

And take the pain
Feel the emotion
The shame
And accept it
As part of you
The way it used to be
And it's like

You thought you'd moved on
From all that
But these moments catch you
Every so often
And you wonder
If maybe
Nothing's changed
At all…

Then what's the point of trying to get better? Why try?

Weathered

Her heart felt heavy
As the clouds do
When they retain too much water.

But life goes on
And soon the rain falls.

Stripped

August 16, 2017

Ed is a demon. Anorexia stripped me and robbed me of…
Of my dignity
Of my youth
Of my happiness
Of my self-worth
Of my appetite
Of my favorite foods
Of my summers
Of my friends and social life
Of my trust in anything or anyone
Of my sleep
Of my honesty
Of my innocence
Of my family's trust
Of my good grades
Of my hope and reasons to live
Of my passion for doing things
Of my sanity
Of my self-control
Of control over my thoughts and mind
Of control over my behavior
Of my womanhood
Of my mind
Of my muscles
Of my teeth
Of my heartbeat.

April 27, 2017

I spent the day with my boyfriend, Aidan, today. We took the bus back to his house after track practice and we were even home alone for a little bit while his dad went out to get groceries. We made out passionately on his bed then cuddled and watched YouTube. Aidan wore his hot new Abercrombie pants, and his hair was the perfect amount of spikey. He was perfect. He was so hot, so sweet, and so perfect. He held me tight and told me that he really loves me and said I was pretty. It seemed like the perfect day. Key word: *'seemed.'*

He also said something that ruined it for me, and after that happened, I texted Mom to pick me up as early as she could. It all happened when I draped one leg over his body the way he likes when we cuddle. He stroked my leg longingly, saying, "Look at those calves! They're huge!"

I sarcastically responded, "Yeah, totally, ha-ha."

But he said, "No, actually in proportion to your body, they're quite large." And that's the moment when my heart broke.

I weighed myself this morning. 74.9 pounds. The worst part is that even after that, he spent the whole evening hugging me, caring for me, and loving me without even knowing I felt hurt! He hadn't meant "large" as an insult. He just meant to say that my legs looked strong—an admirable quality in the eyes of an athlete like himself.

I wanted to leave the moment he'd said it. Strong or not, any means of taking up space was something I did not want to be associated with. But we still had to eat dinner, which his father had so kindly prepared for us. So I did, how could I be so rude as to decline? I ate my dinner reluctantly and politely, a fire silently ripping through the flesh beneath my clothes. To make matters even worse, Aidan made a joke during dinner to his dad that I eat more food than him (he was used to watching me prepare extravagant meals for myself while he was at my house, which I, also bulimic, would later throw up). I forced a fake smile, asked for seconds, and thanked his father for the meal. I held it together for another hour after that until my mom finally came to bring me home, the whole time steaming with bitterness at Aidan's ignorance.

So thanks. Thanks for the compliments. 'I'm so fucking fat. I feel disgusting. Fuck this perfect day, I wish it didn't even happen. And by the way, if I'm so strong, this is the reason why, not my running muscles.'

Silver Lining

A metaphor for optimism; the good side of bad times. A small glimmer of hope; a crack of sunshine in the eye of the storm.

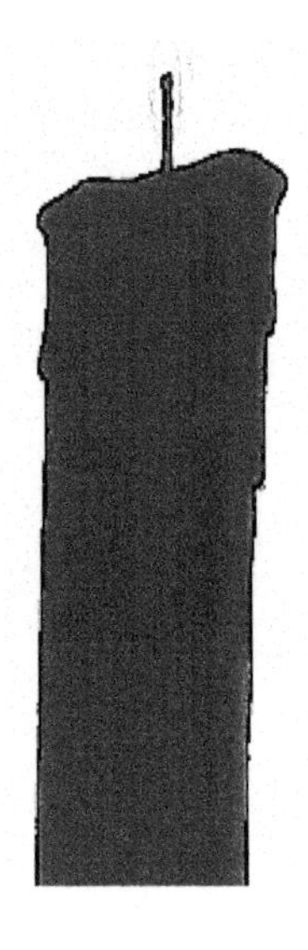

I met Aidan, and my heart started beating again. He made me want to be normal: want to eat dinner with his family, want to go to restaurants and theaters, want to have energy, want to go dancing and laugh my heart out. And little by little, he taught me to do all those things even while knowing how hard it all was for me as a lethargic, anorexic, anxious high school girl. Aidan himself wasn't enough to pull me out of the rut I was stuck in, but he made it so that I wasn't alone.

My Heart

December 30, 2017.

You make my heart smile
More importantly though
You keep it beating.

Liking Someone

Do you ever
Not care about
Someone
Then
One day
All a sudden
You see them in a new light
And slowly
All their flaws fade away
And you find new and
Beautiful things
In them every day
Until it's not slow anymore
And it's only been
Two weeks
And you
Like them
Like really like
Them
And three months later
You love them
And you wonder
How you ever didn't love them
Before
Because they're
Like
The most lovable person
And you're just

You.
But with them
You're somebody.

VOPP

December 28, 2017

He tilted his head and looked at me
With those deep blue, striking, and questioning eyes of his
And called me his "VOPP."

"What? Ha-ha, I don't understand."

"Very Own Personal Princess."

First Love

"I think"
She said
"I *love* that boy
The one who dances in the stars…
With icy eyes
And straw-like hair
And his voice…
Like milk and honey…"

"The one who plucks the tears
From my cheeks
As if he were picking roses…"

"Who talks so smooth
I could drink his words
Like hot chocolate…
He tastes like hot chocolate too…"

An Eclipse

The stars blinked
The sky was gray with charcoal clouds
Splattered with the ink of midnight
She was an eclipse
In this overly ordinary world
She had hair the color of death
And eyes like ice
Her skin as pale as the moon…
But her heart was pure gold
And I, watching her dance barefoot
On grass's glittering dew
Could've started fires with what I
Felt for her.

My palms grew sweaty
My chest ached
The smoke clouded my lungs
Like the sky above
And flames tickled my feet
Until I was dancing too!
I was choking too much
On the smoke
To say anything
But she knew
When she touched my sweaty palm.

Kiss in the Rain

December 8, 2017

I could win the lottery
And
Get my dream job
And
Live in a big, fancy house
With ivy on the walls
Just like I've always wanted
And
Own a thousand different sequin dresses
Like a real princess
Just like I'd always wanted to be
And still
I'd never be close to as
Happy
As I was
When you kissed me
On that rainy sidewalk
One random August afternoon
And told me I was beautiful.

Him

He was that guy with that name who always got mentioned by my friends.

Then he was that annoying kid in History with blond hair and too many things to say.

Then he was that guy who complimented my hair in the hallway, and I thought about it for the rest of the week.

Then he was that guy who frequently made awkward eye contact with me in History.

Then he was that guy I stealthily tried to sit next to at lunch.

Then he was officially my crush.

Then he was my Christmas present to myself
I asked him out
Then he was my boyfriend.

He was my first date.

Then he was my first kiss.
And my first New Year's Eve kiss.

Then he was my boyfriend who frequently made awkward eye contact with me in History.

Then he was the first guy to tell me he loved me. And the first time I said “I love you” back without meaning it.

But soon enough he was the first time I said “I love you” to a guy and really meant it.

Smile

December 30, 2017

My heart gives
        A little jump

Every time
        You smile.

Real Medicine

Best cures for sadness: laughter, chocolate, music, friends, and, of course, therapy.

Falling

December 31, 2017

Her:
"I fell a thousand times over again for you today."

Him:
"I never stopped falling."

Star Boy

The Star Boy
Reached inside her chest
And grasped her little heart…
But was surprised by what he touched
It was rough
With a thousand stitches
It was leaking
And disheveled
But was in one piece
More or less…

"Why"
He inquired the pretty girl
"Are you always so smiley
When you
Don't feel happy inside?"

And she replied
"I put on a brave face
And bottle up my pain
Because I wish someday to be
Who I pretend I am"

"No
It is not the light
Of the stars
That makes them
Beautiful

It's the darkness
Of the sky
That makes them bright

Without pain there is
No happiness.

Be who you are
Be you lonely, sad, or a complete mess
Be it because you *are* it
And don't be anyone else.

I didn't
Fall in love with you
For your smile
I fell in love with you
For your heart
It's a total mess
Just like you, and
I love it
I love you
To the moon and back."

To Be Loved

I'm on my way there
Slowly
And I thank you
For the
Nights
You held me tight
Wrapped me up
In your sweatshirt
And told me to live
Live—"If for no other reason"
You said
"Do it for me"
I want to
And I swear I'm
Trying
Honestly.

And even so
Someday
I wish to love myself
All by myself.

“Fat Attack”

A panic-attack-like experience, characterized by sweaty palms, headache, violent crying, heart palpitations, and staggered breath. Usually described as accompanying an intense, overwhelming feeling of guilt, shame, and insecurity around physical appearance. A term coined by my therapist, Lindsay. She uses it to explain the unpredictably firesome nature of anorexic and bulimic patients who suffer from body dysmorphia during and after recovery from severe weight loss.

Desperate

July 23, 2016

You know the feeling when you really, really, really, really need to go to the bathroom, and you're trying not to think about waterfalls, but of course that's all you can think about? And that uncontrollable shaking and vibration of your leg muscles and pelvis as you cross your legs and squeeze tight? *I will not pee myself. No. Stop*...and you can't even if you wanted to because you're in the car, stuck in traffic... The utter helplessness and embarrassment and shame of it all...

I would, *'without a doubt,'* rather have that feeling *'for the rest of my life'* than to have another *'fat attack. Never ever again. Please.' That is how terrifying it is.*

Rock Bottom

January 22, 2017

Fat attacks are the literal bane of my existence, and yet I cannot run nor hide from them. I can try to cope; I can address the external stressors, etc. But for roughly three years, two months, and two weeks now, I've been suffering fat attacks. That's roughly 1,170 days! That's over a thousand fat attacks! Likely a thousand and a half! Or two thousand! Yet I never get used to it. It gets me every time, and every time my heart breaks in the same place.

How the fuck does Lindsay, how the hell can I, expect my heart to heal after it's been broken so many goddamn times?! Every time, the same place. Stitches torn then re-stitched. After a while, they just don't hold anymore. Like how Mom can't sew my blankey from when I was a baby anymore because he's been sewn too many times before and is just so delicate now that the stitches of the fragile cloth fall apart even more so.

For me, each little stitch is me recovering from the last fat attack, thinking I'm starting to get better. But feeling like I have a chance at getting better just makes me feel worse in the long run. Because it then hurts when I rip myself into fucking pieces all over again. If I never got stitched back together, then technically, I wouldn't have to feel them getting ripped out every time. I'd just be an open wound of a girl. You know? Or like in falling down the stairs, why should one bother climbing back up every time just to set up for a higher fall the next inevitable time?

Why the fuck do I keep bothering to see go to therapy and watch my food intake and try meditation and all that other crap? Why do I try and try and try and try so fucking hard even when I know it isn't working? Why bother recovering if I keep falling back to rock bottom? What if I just stayed there? What if I just lived on rock bottom? It seems like I already am.

Her Killer

"Sticks and stones
May break my bones
But words can never hurt me"
She said.

And *Ed* whispered back:

"We'll prove her wrong
We'll hang her
By her own very words
She'll never see it coming
The very letters
Will prick her fingers
And sentences will strangle
Be it not the language of others
That beats her to the ground
But the voice of her mind
That drowns her
When nobody else
Is around."

Jeans

November 22, 2017

It's that feeling
Of trying on a new pair of jeans
That you were so excited
To order
Because they're just the color and cut
You needed
To go with that pretty top
You don't know what to do with.

It's that feeling
Of being so embarrassed even though
You're alone in your bedroom, for
When you put them on for
The first time
Waves of
It's okay, they just need to be stretched out
And
Did I gain weight?
And
Surely, I must've ordered the wrong size, crash over you
But really
It's all just guilt
Guilty
Of the waist pinching your hips
Of the upper thighs being too tight
And you can feel the denim
Squeezing your thighs
Making you feel enormous

And
Of the way you have to
Roll up the bottoms
Because
They're too long
And you're guilty
Of not being tall enough or thin
Enough, and
You didn't intend to let yourself down
Like this
When you treated yourself
To online shopping
But here you are
Guilty
And overflowing out of your new jeans.

A 'fat attack'
Is
This feeling
Of suffocation and guilt
While you're not even wearing clothes.

It's overflowing out of your own skin
It's pinching your arms
To see if your fingers go all the way around
And they don't
It's sitting on the floor
To get a better angle of your legs
And seeing the sack of fat
Handing off the backs of your thighs
It's squatting like a hip-hop model

To see if your thighs fold evenly
Over your calves
But instead of a straight line
You have a wave
Of the fat on the back of your calves
And your thighs overflowing
On each side of them.
It's telling yourself
It's gonna be okay It's gonna be okay It's gonna be okay It's gonna be okay It's gonna be okay It's gonna be okay It's gonna be okay
But in your head you know
It's happening again It's happening again It's happening Again It's happening again It's happening again It's Happening again It's happening again
And you're trying too hard
You're shaking
Trying to block out
The noise
Erupting over your
Like trying not pee when you've been holding it for several minutes or an hour
Or like
Choking on puke, trying not to explode
Or like
When your heart breaks
And you can feel it literally
Pang in your chest and sting like frostbite
And in essence
This wave
Like a thousand oceans

This volcano
Like Mt. Fuji
Erupts over you
Whether you like it or not
And the lava
Streaks down your face land burns
Oh wait,
Are those tears?
And *the noise*
Strangles you
While you're treading on
The sudden but familiar
Uncertainty of your sanity
And
You're on your tiptoes
Straining every muscle in your body
Trying to keep your head above water
As you drown in thoughts
You drown in *the noise*
The noise
The noise
You've gained weight
How could you do this to yourself?
What the actual fuck is wrong with you
Do you have no self-control?
You were too easy on yourself
You slipped up
Stop trying to be better, it'll never work anyway
You're killing yourself
Stop ruining your progress
I can't go out like this

Ew, I don't want Aidan to touch me
I don't want anyone to see the fat on my legs
I hate the feeling of being heavier
What is this? Please...
Make it stop
I promise I'll do better
I'll starve the next few days I promise
Just please make this noise go away
And
Now I have to live with this
Wretched, bloated feeling
For the rest of the day
And it's only noon
I promise I won't eat anything else today
Please someone come and rescue me
From the depths of my bedroom
But please don't look at me.

It's been said
That anorexia is more
Similar to an alcohol addiction
Than to something like OCD
I can testify to that
For years I've been drunk on the
False euphoria
Of starving
And when I make an effort
To get better
By not starving
The voices in my head grow louder and louder
The noise the noise the noise

And
I experience a sort of
Withdrawal
Form the euphoria
From the control
From the authority
And soon
The same way an addict may
Be craving drugs or alcohol
The noise quickly
Drowns out my positive thoughts
And the advice from my parents
And therapist Lindsay
And my boyfriend Aidan
Until, even though I'm surrounded by
People who love me
I'm all alone in my head
And soon I can't hear anything
But *the noise the noise the noise*
Growing louder and louder
And how am I supposed to go to school
And learn things
And use my brain effectively
If I can't even hear
My chemistry teacher
Over *Ed!*

All I want is a little peace and quiet
But all I've known for the
Past four years
Been *noise noise*

Noise noise.

Being anorexic
Is like that feeling
Of someone talking at you
When you don't want to hear it
It's trying to silently get by in
A heavily noise-polluted life
And it's a constant battle
To hear even
Your own thoughts
Over *the noise*,
Let alone anybody else's.

Sickness

A state of being ill—physically or mentally—and in need of medicine, care, and lots of blankets. Tea and oranges are recommended.

The Decay

My eyes are fogged over like
April's windowpane
They were once twinkling stars
Now deadened by pain.

My nails are yellow
My teeth are gray
My hair's falling out
But I never liked it anyway.

I miss my friends
I miss my smile
I haven't laughed
In quite a while.

And as my heart
Slows its beat
And quiets the drum
Inside of me
I ask myself
If I dare to live…
Could I bear the burden?
Will God forgive?

The Reality of Suffering

It's a beautiful day the sky is sunny

But she is in her room.

She looks in the mirror
And the glass shatters
She doesn't know what to do
Her palms grow sweaty
Her heart beats faster
It tears—it rips—in two.
.

The birds are chirping happily.

Mind spinning
Staggered breaths
Tears, headache, hungry
And *Ed* is watching
His words suffocate the air
And their meanings
Strangle.

The flowers are just beautiful outside.

Ed rapes her
He will hang her
He will kill her
With consent.

A happy family outside strolls by, laughing
But she can’t hear them
Over the voices inside.

He will starve her
Beat her
Blame her
Kill her.

She will die
A slow
And painful
Death.

While the clouds outside
Are fluffy and white.

He will kill her
She will die
She will die
Die
Die inside.

And the sunset will be beautiful.

True Sadness

Do you ever just
Cry so much
That you
Cry yourself dry
Literally
And you're still crying
But there are no tears left
So you're just lying there
In fetal position
Alone
On your bed
Sobbing violently
Silently
And you look like someone who's either
Laughing really hard
Or having a seizure
And
Your head hurts
From crying
And
You're dehydrated now too
And
Once you get your breath under control
You just lay there
Calm, Motionless
Defeated
And contemplate the world
And think about

Your life
And how much of it
You’ve spent
Just
Crying.

The Burning

"I am afraid"

She whispered to me.

"I walk around everyday
With fire in my lungs
Flames peek out from beneath my clothes…

"I'm afraid to be alone with my own mind
Vulnerable to attack
Where I may be
Burned alive
By my own emotions
Chewed up
And
Swallowed
By the flames…"

Coconuts

The best way I can describe anorexia is that it's *innocent…* In the beginning. It starts out with a simple goal: to be healthier or to lose just a couple pounds. But then, it spirals out of control. And it's all because of the *noise*… Every time you reach your goal weight, you decide you can lose a little more instead of stopping. Then *noise noise noise noise noise noise noise noise* you're not getting enough nutrients to your brain, so you get a little bonkers and it's like a light swithes off *noise noise noise noise noise* in your brain or some chemical reaction *noise noise noise noise noise* and you physically can't see yourself for who or what you actually are and that's when *Ed* takes over *noise noise noise noise noise noise noise noise noise noise* bcuease peolpe see you as what are but in the mriror *noise noise noise noise noise* you are literally someone else who Only you can see.

So then, people around you start getting worried, So you have to be mroe discreet about dieting *noise noise noise noise noise.* And *noise noise noise noise noise noise noise noise noise noise* this is wehre all the lies and heartbreak cmoe in and you're so frustrated bceuase you don't udnrestnad. Why *noise noise noise noise noise?* Ervynoe can't just leave you aonle?

You aren't even siknny! noise Noise noise noise noise If aynythnig, you're fat and you're drwnoing in your own Skin and noise noise *noise.* then the dtocros tell you that if You don't stop dientig *noise noise noise noise noise* you may acquire Irreversible Damage *noise noise noise noise noise* so it feels like you have to choose between being happy and skinny *noise noise noise noise noise* and not gtetnig panic attacks *noise noise noise noise noise* vesus settling for a lfie of a prsoen who's meant to be fat. noise noise noise noise noise.

is being fat the only way i can be healthy? why me? why can some popele survive bineg skinny and i can't? noise noise noise noise noise noise i don't want this life of noise noise noise noise noise noise. if seeing dtocros and haivng fat attacks is what life is, *then maybe i just don't want to live.* this life is so fucking noisey.

And There mghit come a day wehn you say *that* to your mom and noise noise noise noise noise. She cries and noise noise noise noise noise. You feel like You shulod feel bad for Her, but you can't feel aytnhing because noise noise noise noise noise your brain is so noisey and numb noise noise. So, you and noisey noise just sit in your bed All day. you cry. You think *noise noise noise* you're giong to die because you've gvien *noise noise* up on life, But that's Not how biology works. noise Just because noise noise you give up noise deson't mean *noise* your body does; noise won't give up you. so N*oise NOise NOIse NOISe NOISE noisE noiSE noISE nOISE NOISE noise.*

You get help one-way or aonther maybe, thanks to good ole Mom. You tihnk everything will be OK once you've pyhsilacaly recovered (a.k.a. put on weight) … Right?! Right?! WRONG. Just *noise noise* because *noise* the ntrueintns *noise* noise *noise* noise are flowing *noise* to your brain aagin noise noise noise noise noise noise. and *noise* noise noise noise even if you Eat *noise* cnostentisly *noise noise* for several mohtns. Months of noise. That doesn't maen Your brian noise noise noise noise suddenly sees yuroelsf the way it soluhd. Your brain is enmtoilaly scarred by noisey noisey *Ed.* SorRy for the spoiler, but You will still get pnaic atactks even after pyhscially rcovernig. *noise noise* Your mnid is peppered with dstoritoin and shmae and you suffer from noise noise noise noise and cnfuison and fursttioran *noise* noise noise noise and so much *noise* in the benigning that it might not feel wroth it to even try to eat if it doesn't chnage aynhtnig noisey.

But it does! This is wehre your bravery shines. Now is the time to snik or swim. You'll prbaboly recover then relapse over and over again and noise noise noise noise noise noise noise noisE I'm sorry, *noise noise.* But all I can relaly say *noise noise noise noise* Is that one day you'll be lvinig the life you wished for when you were a little kid and You'll be laughing at *Ed* for eevn thinking that for mnomnet he had a chnace at taking you.

Either that, or noise noise noise noise noise noise noise noise noise noise you'll be dead, hopefully in Heaven, Although I'm pretty sure self-harm is a Sin. Hopefully you didn't take anyone down with you, like your friends. I hope you raise people up and Once you recover, reach out to thsoe who are struggling and pull them out of the drkasens they are drowning in. Teach them how to swim.

Then Maybe One Day, Everyone will find shore and we'll all eat coconuts and mangoes together on the Island. I'm an atheist at this point, but I'll pray for it. I'll pray for us.

A Big Black Ocean

November 2, 2017

I am barely
Treading water
In this big black ocean we call *Human Consciousness.*

Eggshells

November 20, 2017

You've fallen
Out of your nest, out of your life, and out of love
And all the memories and
All your hard work up to this point
Along with your heart, has been smashed
Like a fragile egg on a concrete surface.

And now the once potential you held
As a young chick is slowly oozing out
Onto the pavement
All the hopes and dreams smashed
By a strong arm with a firm grip
And a vengeful conscience.

His name was *Ed*
Or Depression or Guilt or Society
Or whatever you want to name him
But what you name him doesn't matter
So much as the fact that
He happened.

And everyone's got a different story to tell
About how they ended up here on the concrete
But as the story goes
There are more smashed eggs in this parking lot
Than cars, and I
C can't remember now whether I even fell.

From a literal nest, or if I was just caught up
In another one of my metaphors
Because I've been down here so long that
Mu insides have all dried to the pavement
Like a sugary drink on a hot day
Left out on the porch by a little one.

And I'm starting to question
Whether we even have lives at all
Or if we all came from a basket
Held by that meaty hand
And there wasn't ever really
A choice.

We like to tell ourselves that this is all an accident
That we were the unlucky ones
But do we actually have any evidence
That we were ever even meant to fly with slimy wings?
This whole time I've been thinking my parents
Were blue jays.

But maybe the world knew already
From before I ever existed
That my life was meant to be smashed on the concrete
I don't know, it's just that I just realized how all the shells
on this ground are thin and white
Like grocery store eggs…

Trapped

The state of being stuck in a particular space or circumstance with no escape.

Addiction

The lowest weight I ever reached in my teenage years was 67 pounds when I had just turned 14 years old. Throughout the summer of 2014, I rigidly maintained a BMI of almost 15. In early August, I was finally scrutinized and given an ultimatum by my parents and one of my doctors. Essentially, there were legal concerns that my parents would be sued by that state if I didn't recover soon enough because their lack of control over the situation was considered neglectful parenting. So, my doctor drew up a contract which indicated a requirement that I gain five pounds by the coming October. If I failed to comply, I would promptly be sent to a facility. Honestly, I probably would have recovered a lot quicker had I just checked into the hospital, but my parents were adamant about not losing their custody of me to the state, which was up in the air as an option by that point.

This subject was broached to me by my dad one hot summer afternoon on the back porch, just after I'd finished half a slice of bread with a 0.25cm thick layer of strawberry jam on top for lunch. Honest to God, it felt like the end of the world. What started out as an expectedly bitter conversation turned into a total meltdown on my part. I cried there in a plastic deck chair for the rest of the afternoon thinking through my life and what I would look like as a grandma if I kept this up, and if I'd ever even become a grandma. Well, I reasoned, I'm either going to look like Grammy on Mom's side—horribly frail and depressed—or like Grandma on Dad's side—long gone and dead. Yet, I refused to stop losing weight. It was the only thing keeping *'the noise'* out…the insufferable voice in my head constantly criticizing every ounce of flesh on my body.

Before I'd ever taken a psychology course in my life, I was telling always telling myself: "Sex, food, sleep. We all have our addictions. Mine just happens to be losing weight." And I would remain imprisoned by my addictions the same way an alcoholic is chained to the bar; this was the reality, but also my justification. I believed that the world was innately bad and that f everyone else was already killing themselves slowly then all I was doing was doing it better and faster—I was winning. That's why everyone was trying to stop me, I thought. But more than even that, dieting was a coping mechanism for the depression such beliefs had planted within me. As a young teen, you're too old to be a kid but too young to make your own decisions; it feels like you don't have control over anything in your life. Controlling my weight and my eating gave me power. It gave me a corrupt authority over my parents which I could then dangle over their heads to get whatever I wanted. And most importantly, beyond all food fights and trivial allowances, the one thing I needed most, which anorexia granted me, so I thought, was the ability to control death. The death that was slowly killing everyone, the one I was running at. Anorexia took away the terror of inevitable death. By planning my own, I never had to be afraid it. I expected it and welcomed it drowsily with open arms like weak and tree branches.

Threads

October 15, 2017 – 7:44 a.m.

My body:
Is an array of a thousand threads
Criss-crossed several times
In several messy attempts to
Stitch my broken pieces back together
Again and again and
At this point, things are connected in all the wrong places
And I don't know me any better than you do.

Me, every morning:
Please sun, make your journey across the sky
Hastily:
I am waiting anxiously
For the evening birds' lullaby
So that
Finally, gratefully
I may retire to blissful unconsciousness.

I'm the one:
Who takes seven different pills every night
Just to stay whole
Who walks on life as if it were
Hot coals
Whose smile is as bright as her mind is dark
Who wears masks as often
As if they were socks.

My stomach:

Is forever guilty
Of not being
Empty enough
No matter for how
Many years
I've
Starved.
My mind:
Is the nucleus of all my
Suffering
A factory for corrupt thoughts
With blue and gray colorings
All of them broken record players
Repeating *Ed*'s voice
Relentlessly.

I live:
On the shoreline of
An endless sea
Of nightmares
And I'm scared
That one day
I may literally
Drown in it.

Leaves

October 25, 2017

I am a wet leaf
Of autumn
Stuck to the pavement
And slowly losing my color.

But no one notices
As they step right over me
Because I blend in with the dozens of others
Who have fallen to the same fate.

Some of them are
The bright red and gold feathers that little girls
Take home to their parents and press in wax paper to keep
Others mingle amongst the acorns and branches besides them.

The ones who are like me
Are the ones who were once
Bright orange fires or big juicy red strawberries
The kinds of leaves you see in Instagram pictures.

But life happens and nature doesn't exclude
The best and worst of us wind up in puddles
And get stuck to the ground gazing up at the murky clouds
Above us.

This is where I have been all season, and
Will continue to be

Because no matter how much the wind blows
I still can't find my way out of this puddle.

I'm stuck to the sidewalk the way
Wet toilet paper succumbs to the weight of moisture
And you know what it does next? It falls apart.

God, I wish I could just disintegrate already.

But no, that is not the way God would have it
I must sit here while everyone, besides a few like me
Play in leaf piles and swim along the autumn breeze
Like red and gold and orange confetti.

I am a watcher of the world. I have seen the sky on its darkest and most cloudy days
And have felt the subtly warmth of
The last rays from fiery sunsets.

I am silent and I am alive and
I am wishing I wasn't and
And
I don't know why
Everyone gets so excited for fall
We are all
Going to die anyway.

I wish I could get out of this depression, but I can't
It's the water holding me here, not me
And I know neither of us can do anything
But wait for the sun to dry the pavement I lay on.

But during these rainy weeks, I ask of you just one thing:
Just please, please, please
Acknowledge me before stepping on me
Some of us need that “hello” just to stay strong.

August 20, 2017

It's Noah's last night at home before we take him to Florida tomorrow for college. Everyone's downstairs, celebrating Noah's September birthday early and eating turkey burgers with Oreo cake. Meanwhile, I haven't eaten since 4 p.m. It's 8:30 now. My arms ache because I just finished an online arm workout. I had to force myself to shower before starting my workout. I'm about to do abs. I have half a six-pack already, but it's mostly just my ribs, which makes it a twelve-pack, I guess. Ha ha. My head feels like a balloon because I've barely drank any water today. I should be downstairs with my family. I should've eaten dinner. But instead, I'm locked away in my room with the lights off, doing sit ups alone with no company but *Ed* on my shoulder, whispering in my ear about how fat my arms are…How I don't want to be seen…How I wish life wasn't this way. *'But it is,'* and I don't even know if Mom or Dad or Noah even know that. Mom texted me from downstairs, asking if I was asleep because they are going to sing to Noah. So I went downstairs and sang, then came back up. Now, I feel unmotivated to do the rest of my workout, and I kind of just want to go to bed. But I'll probably end up doing butt lifts at 10:00 pm. It's now 9:03. I've been awake for 18 hours already today because I woke up at 3:00 a.m. this morning. I don't know if it's my antidepressant medication or what, but I haven't been sleeping well. I'm always too wide awake at night and too depressed and fatigued during the day.

Acorn Street: Part 7: Rice Cakes and Suicide

It was the street on which I took a furious nighttime run, my brain on fire and eyes melting. I was so heartbroken and frustrated because my last straw was long broken, but still my soul was raped hourly by *Ed*. I ran all the way to the pond at the end of the street and screamed to all the earshot trees and flies a threat to drown myself. But I couldn't. So I returned home only to make a show of taking an entire box of rice cakes and crushing them one by one all over the kitchen floor before my kneeling, sobbing father. I fucking hate food.

Seven Stuffed Animals

December 4, 2017

I just have to lay there
With seven stuffed animals in my arms
I have to lay there
And take it
Take the pain
And shake violently
As the years force their way out of my eyes
In drops of water
And the sadness washes over me
Like a shadow.

And there's nothing I can do
Because
When the lights are on
There's a shadow
And when the lights are off
Everything is dark anyway.

Either way
I am doomed to a life
Of mascara stained cheeks
And curling up into a ball
In fetus position
Screaming
Silently
For someone to come rescue me. And
I look at my phone, texting him calmly
About nothing in particular

And

At the same time

I'm shouting through the phone at that oblivious boy

Help me

Please

Help me.

Dream Recollections: A Run

I once had a dream that it was a warm, sunny summer day, and I was on a run along Acorn Street. As I was passing a cute Chinese boy named Brendan's, house, which is on the other end of the street as mine. It suddenly began snowing, and as I ran up the hill toward home, the snow began to fall increasingly heavier, and the sky was darkening with each passing step.

When I reached Riley's house, which is the halfway point of our one-mile street, there was about a foot of snow on the ground, and it was deep black nighttime. I was having trouble running, as my feet were sinking into the snow too much, and I could barely see. I started to think to myself about how I will need Mom to come pick me up and that I will not be able to finish my run. But when I looked down at my shorts, I realized that only then that I was freezing cold. I also noticed that I had no phone to call her with; I had earbuds in my ears for music, but they were tucked into an empty pocket, and at that moment, the music stopped.

Then there was a car, and it began to pull into the driveway just ahead of me. So, I stood on the corner and waved my hands in the air, hoping they would notice me and help me out, and maybe give me a ride back home.

All of the sudden, the person in the car replaced my thoughts as the narrator of the dream; they noted how they saw something in the snow but couldn't quite make out what it was through the storm. As they were talking, I watched the foggy yellow blobs of the car's headlights moving closer. When the car stopped right in front of me, I saw the driver of the car squint at me, trying to figure out what was going on, but the snow peppered their window, and it was difficult for them to see.

Yet another surprise was when, just then, my foot fell through the snow upon which I was standing, and I collapsed into the snow. I sunk onto my knees in the snowbank, still in my runners' spandex and running shoes. It almost felt as though I would pass out at this point, but I didn't. I just sat on my knees in the snow, with a slightly twisted ankle that was beginning to sting with frostbite. The snow on my legs pierced my skin with utter cold—a burning sensation.

The driver's voice spoke again, wondering aloud if the moving shape they saw through their foggy window was human or some sort of animal. This was startling for me to hear, because I had previously assumed that they knew I was a person. Although I knew they couldn't clearly see me, I thought they would be thinking more about what I wanted from them and why I was waving my hands in the air. That moment proved to be quite scary and unsettling for the both of us—as suddenly I myself was unsure whether I was an animal or a human or a bush or merely a shadowy figure. The voice concluded that I was a dark creature from Hell, and at that idea, both of us screamed out of surprise at the same moment, further fueled by each other's terror.

Not more than a moment later, my acquaintance suddenly shrugged it off and drove on, as if their memory had been wiped, and they'd never seen me at all, calmly pulling into the driveway of their cozy abode and leaving me stranded and alone.

I never made it home, for my dream abruptly ended.

July 25, 2017 – 3:04 P.M.

It's
Feeling like you have nowhere to go.

It's locking yourself in your room and hiding under your bed.

It's
Skipping school because you don't want anyone to see you
But you still muster up the courage to go to the gym instead
Because you know the anxiety will only amplify as the night goes on unless you get moving.

It's
Been raining all day. It's the feeling of wishing you could appreciate
The smell of the rain and the dewdrops on the windows, but all you can think about is how it prevents you from going walking outside. It prevents you from burning calories.

It's
Letting the darkness of the sky cast its shadow over you and envelop you. Letting it depress you.

Existing vs Living

October 29, 2017

Existing
Is
Waking up
Every single day
And wishing
You didn't.

Living
Is
Waking up early
To watch the sunrise
And keeping as many as you can
In your back pocket
Before it's time to go.

Thump, Thump, Thump

I dive into an
Ocean of darkness
And inhale deeply
To fill my lungs
With the black water
And suffocate
The
Excruciating beat
Of the drum inside my
Chest.

I hate the
Wretched, shameful
Sound
Of that broken
Drum beating
Might as well
Discard it
While my ears are not
Yet
Bleeding.

Headspace

Dec 14, 2017

The flame of a candle
Being suffocated
As you put the lid back on.

A tree surrounded by concrete
Inhibiting its growth
Up and to the sides
So that it may still be growing
Thanks to the soil beneath its trunk
But it can only grow *in on itself*
Then
You take away the rain
For good measure.

A man stuck in a chimney.

Wearing heavy earphones
For several hours
Listening to the same
Explicit track
On repeat
And then
Someone tells you to take them off
And
Your ears can now breathe in
The glorious buzz of the refrigerator
In the otherwise silent room
Like lying, floating on water

Slightly dazed, slightly infinite
Utter bliss.

Persistence

You must keep going. I know it really, really sucks, and that is really, really cliché, but it's the only advice I have even after all these years of experience. Please. Do. Not. Give. Up.

The Garden: Part One

The Garden of
Eden
Was all an illusion
As I walked
Through the beautiful graveyard
The charming earth greeted me
With black dirt, decaying smells…
Roses as red as blood
Sunflowers smiling their
Ignorant smiles
Like the type of girls
Who are always beaming
Because they have no idea what's going on
The clouds were lint balls in the sky
Not animals or shapes to look at
I saw no boats or tigers or faces
That day in Eden
But the clouds cried and their tears
Fed the Garden
The mangled roots beneath my wellies
Swallowed the drink thirstily

And
Greedily.

The Garden: Part Two

Sick honeysuckles droop from tired stems
Like dewdrops threatening to drip from skeletal branches
Snakes that coil upon themselves like slow slithering spirals
Slither from leaf to rock and take in the mudded earth
Fog suffocates the Garden and clouds my vision
The wind whispers in my ear
That beautiful things are not always what they appear.

Do not look at this garden in all its beauty
For life doesn't bloom every single second
And sadness exists
You can't always drink the sweetness of the air like raw honey
Life isn't always fair and girls aren't always pretty…

Life isn't always fair and
Girls aren't always pretty
But they don't need to be
The Garden wasn't planted to sprout eye candy
And inspire bird songs
Not every garden is the perfect wedding backdrop
Or Monet painting
Some gardens weren't planted at all
They were born to be mangled
And wild
And dirty
And beautifully unorganized.

A Wilted Petal

Tears like raindrops
Speckle a petal cheek
She is delicate
She is a flower
She cries because she cannot bloom
There are no April showers.
Her days are gray, her heart is cold
She wishes for better days. But the clouds gather
Like flies to light
And sadness
Never
Goes
Away.

Heaven

August 3, 2017

Living with anorexia and depression for several years now, I've felt so alone and so hopeless for an entire four years—a fourth of my lifespan, which makes it easy to feel as though, sometimes, nothing matters and there's no point in living. You may or may not be surprised to hear that I contemplate death a lot. I spend a lot of time just lying in bed, listening to sad music and extensively planning my funeral. Obviously, that's not productive for a depressed person. Of course, I know that. But sometimes, it's all I can do to cope. *'I don't have a choice.'* I picture my family there, greeting people at the head of the church. I listen to heartbreaking music and picture you there, in a sharp black suit, and I feel so guilty for doing that to you. The wreckage on your face says it all. How could I do this to you? You told me I was the only thing that made you *'feel feelings,'* and I took that away from you, like blowing out a candle, then left you with the numbness of your life before I came along. I look on at myself in the casket, and I wish it didn't have to be that way. Not for myself, but because you told me once that *dying doesn't end the pain, it just passes it onto others*. I don't want to hurt the ones I love most. I don't want you to grieve for me.

Of course, it's a formal-Catholic funeral because my family is formal and Catholic. But 'religious' or 'not religious' are just words. They're just labels, like saying you are white or American or speak English or vegetarian or lactose intolerant. With regards to the idea of God and Heaven, it's not that I believe in it, but it allows me to reason that people I love, will be in good hands even if I screw up and throw away my own life. Or at least, that's what I tell myself. I'm not afraid of death because I'm afraid of not existing; I'm afraid of death because I'm afraid of *the 'world around me'* not existing. I'm afraid of never seeing my family again and never seeing my friends and never seeing Aidan again. It may be years or who knows how long between the times that they and I die, but at least I know I'll see them again someday.

I'm not claiming that Heaven is real, but I hypothesize that the point of it being represented by a physical place in the sky it is that it allows people to picture it. If people just called it 'resting in peace' or something instead of 'Heaven,' then it wouldn't be as effective because you'd be peaceful, but non-existent and without conscience. You'd be alone. I don't know about you, but I want to see my grandpa again. I want to see my grandma and my parents and you again one day.

Views (Part 1): The Gray

I look into her eyes
They are ironically blue
For her sky never is
They sparkle like wet rocks on the shoreline
Glistening in the sun. *Sigh, irony*
The sun hides from her
Behind lint gray clouds
Her eyes are tired, weathered from the many tears
They've cried
Yet somehow, they keep leaking.

Every time
It's for the same reason
Yet it gets her every time
Like how some lucky people fall in love
With their partner every day.

Her heart has scars
For it breaks in the same place
Every time
Her days smell of stale air and anxiety
The days are long
Like her eyelashes.

And at the end of each one
The gray sky drags the sun
Down until there is no light at all
She cries at night when the quiet is loud enough

To mask her staggered breath and dark enough
That nobody can see her closed eyes crying.
And the tears hovering in their corners
As she eventually
Escapes into sleep.

Views (Part 2): Dreams

She has dreams of better times.

She lusts for light pink skies
(Her favorite color)
With rose gold sunrises
And a buttermilk sun
And rays like tinsel
That tickle her skin with
The warmth of summer.

There are clouds, too
But not like the
Ones that currently pile
Weight on her shoulders
Like stacks of rocks
The clouds she dreams of are
Not charcoal.

But pure white
Like sheep prancing
Through a pink field of
Endless sky
And if they ever were to stack up
It wouldn't be like rocks
It'd be like
Pancakes on Sunday morning.

But enough about clouds, for she dreams of more than skies.

She dreams of
Monday mornings
With music and breakfast
She dreams of Friday nights
With friends and dancing
She dreams of drinking chocolate on
Winter nights, and red pajamas.
She dreams of better days
When she'll be able to
Listen to upbeat music
Instead of the sad harmonies
That currently moan in her ears
She wants to sing
Her own songs.

Instead of wearing $300
Sound-reduction headphones
In attempt to block out the sounds
Of her dinner guests' chewing
But which only amplifies
The noise of her
Buzzing mind.

She dreams of a life
Of content
In which
One day
Her eyes will be just as shiny
And beautiful
Not from sadness, but from joy.

Maybe tears of joy.

But she wants to stop crying
She wants to stop regretting
And hurting
And fighting.

The Gray Area

December 11, 2017

Depression is funny
Because you're stuck in this gray area
Some sort of in-between solid and liquid
Kind of like
That pencil sitting around
In your pencil case
Quietly awaiting its undetermined fate
Because it's grown far too dull
To write effectively with
And yet
You're too lazy to go sharpen it
So, it just chills there
Trying not to freak out
Yet at the same time
Feeling nothing at all.

Tears of Joy

She was wishy washy
Her legs turned to water
Her knees shook.

Her cold breath was staggered
Like ocean waves
Uncertainty and unruliness
Power and noise
It fills her lungs and swallows her up
The sadness, that is.

And her eyes darted like dragonflies
Across a pond
They were glassy
Then they fell out!
They began to melt
Her eyes started leaking
And her tears
Hit the black earth beneath
Her worn feet.

She stood there
In the garden
Shaking violently
As the waterfall came.

But the tears didn't drown her
This time.

They washed her face
And watered the parched earth
Upon which she stood.

The sun watched the whole thing
From behind a cloud, and
When it was sure she wasn't looking
It came out
And her tears grew into flowers
That tickled her feet.

She knew
At last
This was not a sad-cry
But a cleansing.

These were tears of joy.

If God Isn't Real

December 14, 2017

I may not believe in God
But I believe in Faith.

I believe in helping hands and
Sappy Valentine's Day cards
I believe in good people with
Pure hearts
Hiding in the corners of the earth
Like small green sprouts
Growing between the cracks of concrete sidewalks
I believe in climbing new mountains everyday
Even if you always wake up at rock bottom.

And I believe in miracles.

I believe in the way you manage to say a thousand words
With the wink of an eye
And the warmth of your hand in mine
I believe in the lack of air in my lungs
When you squeeze me tight
And the likelihood that it will happen again.

I believe in roughing the storm
Even when everyone around you is silently drowning
Because I believe in the way the
Sun
Keeps coming back out, again and again
Following each brutal storm

Much like a human heart
Which keeps on beating
After breaking over and over again.

And
Still, through it all, *there is Faith.*

Three Minutes

December 14, 2017

It's listening to a new song
And feeling like it was written
Just for you
Like the ice around you
Suddenly melts
And
Bursts of light
And
Beams of sunlight
Come rushing
Exploding
Out of your chest
And
Your eyes glaze over
With a thin, shimmering layer of tears
Of relief
Because finally
Someone
Put to music
Everything you never said.

And finally
Your head is above water
For a brief three minutes
Because
Even though
You're alone with your headphones and
The tapping of your foot

At least
You know that there are people out there
Who know
The feeling of those thoughts in your head
That you'd always assumed were *only* in you.

Because the music
Makes everything
A little less scary
As your demons are painted against
And empowering ballet
And
Sweet notes reverberate through you
Each one like a drop on honey
In an all-too-bitter world.

And so
You just sit there
Listening
Emotional and reflective
About life.

And
You run your fingers through your hair and
Look out
The car window
Longingly
Starting off into the vast distance
As if
You're the star of the imaginary music video
For this song

For but a blissful three minutes.

And
Each time you listen to it again
And again
You feel like
Maybe
You can keep going for another three minutes
And another
Until eventually
It's been months' worth
Of three-minute intervals
Of barely hanging on
To the end of each sentence
Barely above water
But you breathe
The melodies
Like medicine.

And
With each flick of your hair
And
Secret concert in your room at night
And
Every sleepy car ride
You slowly heal. And you move on
And then
The cycle starts again…
Another wave crashes over you
So, you
Put your headphones back in

And
Start another song.

And on life goes.

Your Favorite Old Sweater

December 11, 2017

I am the debris left over from a hundred hurricanes.

I am your favorite old sweater, clearly worn and fraying at the ends of the sleeves and slowly unraveling with each wash.

I am the outcast pieces at the bottom of the cereal box that never get eaten because they fell out of the bag.

I am the slightly numb and tired feeling you get when you take too many Advil for a headache that still won't go away.

I am the stains on your sheets from countless cold, sweat inducing nightmares.

I am the old pictures you can't bear to reminisce over because it gets you too emotional.

I am bruises.

And
Broken records.

And
A mess of threads clumsily holding
All my broken pieces together.

And

I am alive.

And
I am beautiful.

Confession

A truth that would rather not be brought to light because it is a pretext to guilt, shame, or vulnerability. Or, often, all three.

From the Bottom of My Heart

I have a suggestion: break up with Ed. Break up with secrets and lying and hiding uneaten food under your bed. Stop turning on the shower to blur the noise of you throwing up in the toilet. Stop skipping school because your jeans feel tight. Stop throwing a tantrum every time Dad accidentally touches you because now his molecules are multiplying all over your skin, and you need to shower before it causes weight gain.

I'm not even kidding—these are the things I worried about. And the things my parents didn't know about.

Confessions

I bottle things up and
Get passive aggressive
Because
I'm afraid of confrontation
Not because I'm weak, but
Because
I know the power of my words
From past experiences and
I'm fully aware
That
I am very capable of being
Cruel and
Unyielding and
I just don't want to hurt anyone.
It's like those movies
When someone acquires superpowers
Then they're all afraid to touch anyone
Because
They don't want to hurt them…
Don't touch me, stay away! I am dangerous.

Our Broken House

It's the sound of closing doors
And silent screams
"Come back"
But the words drown in an ocean of quiet
That refuses to be disrupted.

There's an unspoken agreement
In this house
Among my family
That we all know each other are
Drowning
Together in this fish tank
We are all lonely
And tired
But irritability is sparks to a match
And if you tease it
Fire will erupt
Like a thousand oceans
Crashing down like cold hard feelings then
Draining into nothingness.

Here in this underwater house
We are
Broken and
Ignorant and
We all refuse
To say that anything is wrong.

Our house is

Friendly on the outside
With a large deck and rows of pear trees
But inside
We each occupy
Our separate corners
Of the house.

Our house
Is overflowing with
Unspoken thoughts
And we are all suffocating
Behind closed doors
Like fish drowning in a pond that
Nobody knew was saturated
With oil.

We're the lonely ones,
Who sit alone in the dark
Who pretend not to notice each other
As each of us
Simultaneously
Wilts away like delicate carnations
In a melting garden
Amidst the parched summer heat.

The Quiet Kid

So, there's this kid who got upset because he's always told he's 'the quiet kid' and everyone always says *'to not be shy'* and *'just be confident* and to *let loose,'* as if he's holding back. But it's frustrating because he's *'not'* holding back! *'Jeez.'* He just doesn't have anything to say. He's still a human being, and he has opinions, ideas, and a brain just like everybody else! He could say that Sam's too nosey, and Stephanie is really cute, and Bret's haircut sucks, and Mrs. Flaherty only has one sock on, and basketball is by far the best sport, but he doesn't. Maybe, everyone gives him such a hard time because they assume that he's dying to tell the world all of this but that he's too shy because it's a human need to express oneself…

But you know what? *'Fuck it.'* Maybe, most people express themselves by talking 85% nonsense 101% of the time, but it's unfair to accuse me of not expressing myself because maybe I already am. I express myself everyday by being the opposite of you. You can all voice your opinions and everything, and all the teachers talk about how *'involved'* and *'outgoing'* you all are, but by not talking, I voice my opinion that humanity doesn't need to be heard 101% of the time. Maybe, humanity should shut up for a change, and see that they're not the only ones on this planet.

My parents are vegans. Jake, you don't need to repeat every word the teacher says in order to understand it. I have straight As. I love origami. My point is? *'Fuck'* expression. *'No, wait, fuck talking, and fuck you.'* Stop calling me *'quiet,'* because when you say that, it makes me feel like you are calling me *'insignificant'* and *'opinion-less.'* There are several other methods of human expression than just verbal output.

Honestly, I express more than you'd ever know if only you stopped talking for a second to notice. **I'm not quiet, you just don't listen.**

Memories

June 21, 2017 – 8:14 p.m.

What did you love about her? The way she saw the world in different colors? The blue of her eyes which glowed like electricity when she cried? Or maybe how she stressed out about ordinary things and pulled you in close when frightened.

How she loved classical music. Or how everyone always said she was cute when she was nervous. How she was clumsy and always dropped her phone and stubbed her toes. How she could trip over perfectly flat floors or how she could light up a room without saying anything.

Maybe how she had the best fashion sense but never said anything about it. She took their compliments with a grain of salt and never fully believed you when you called her beautiful. That drove you crazy, didn't it? Like that night you told her she had 'nice calves…very large and muscular,' and she texted you later that night about how she was going to starve herself until she didn't have calves. Did she make you feel guilty? Or confused? Or infinite?

Like the way she hates silence and needs you to keep talking but never knows what to talk about. Or how you thought she couldn't swim because she refused to touch the water at that pool party last summer, but she *could* swim, she just didn't feel comfortable in her bikini. Did you love her for the way she ran her fingers through your hair? Remember that time? When she did your makeup, and as it turns out, you make a pretty hot woman!

Did you think it was cute when she would wear your glasses in Chemistry, because she secretly needed them? What about when she finally got glasses of her own? You said they were hot. She got the clear framed just like she wanted. And you told her she was right about them.

Isn't it funny how sometimes it feels like you're dating your best friend? Does the thought of it ending break your heart the way it broke hers? Did you even think about that? How often do you cry? You told her you hadn't cried in years. She cried every day. Did you know? How did that make you feel? Like you wanted to help? Or like she was weak?

Was it hot? You told her intelligence is attractive. In fact, you told her that you only date people who are smarter than you because you want them to make you better. Did you think she was smarter than you? You told her so. Did you know that she didn't believe you? Not in a million lifetimes did she feel as good as you. She was stubborn, wasn't she? Just ask her mom, or her grandma, because God knows stubbornness is genetic. Hell yes, in a thousand lifetimes and any version of reality, she was stubborn. You probably wished she stubborn about things more worthwhile than SAT's and dying.

Did you actually think she would get into Harvard? No? Is that why you never let her talk about college? Did you know her dad went there? What if she did get in? Would you be happy for her? Or jealous? Did you ever wonder what her GPA was? Did you know she obsessed over yours? Do you even care? Isn't ironic how smart she was and yet not smart enough to outsmart Ed? Is that natural selection then?

What about when she dyed her hair? Did you know that she did it because she hates how dark it turns in the winter—the way her pale skin makes her look like a vampire—and how she was afraid she might get depressed again if she let herself fall cold to the snow outside? But she did anyway and punished herself by slicing her wrists. Were you horrified by her complaining about the cuts being itchy beneath winter sweaters? Or amused?

Does it irritate you the way teenage girls justify obnoxious behavior with their feelings, like when they're depressed, or they have anxiety? Does that make it okay? You said you hated girls like that. How was she any fucking different?

A Promise I Can't Keep

One day you'll meet someone
Who reaches inside your chest
And effortlessly, perfectly
Steals your heart.

Honestly,

I just want to be okay again.

Twigs

December 11, 2017

I was competing with branches and baby tree trunks for the width of my arms.

Dream Recollections: My Twin Sister

I was a twin.

I had a twin sister when I was very young. I didn't remember because I was young at the time she died, and so my parents just *'never told me.'*

They hid it all away—every picture with her in it—every memory of her pushed to the back of their minds, easy as swallowing a pill. They never...*never* told me I was a twin.

But then, when I grew to be a teenager, maybe 14 or 15 years old, I started experiencing vivid, strange flashbacks of *'her.'* At first, I thought that, perhaps, I was seeing another version of myself or something, but I somehow—within the depths of my memory—uncovered the fact I *was* a 'twin' when I was little.

I got a few friends from school in on the situation, and they agreed that my parents were keeping something from me. It was just an odd feeling.

So then, one day, Mom and Dad were rushing out of the house to go to a dinner party, and I blurted out the question like an unplanned firework shooting off: *"Dad, am I an only child? Was there ever...someone else...?"*

His pupils dilated, he stopped putting on his coat, and broke down crying, one arm halfway into his sleeve, the other covering his face. "*Yes...she passed away a long time ago...Ellie..."*

Just then, with perfect timing, Mom came clunking downstairs in her heels, her pearls and sequin dress, hair freshly dyed, and eyeliner clumping in the inner corners of her aged eyes.

"What's going on here?"

"I was a twin...and you never told me..."

All expression left her face—stone cold—and what followed was the familiar awkwardness about her only familiar to awkward one-sided discussions about puberty.

"We're going to be late. Let's go."

My dad shot me a sympathetic smile and a cautious glace at my mother, then quickly slipped his other arm into his pea coat, and they both rushed out of the house.

I watched the dark blob of their car leave the driveway, turn the corner, and disappear into the winter evening.

While they were gone, three of my most charismatic girlfriends came over...We snooped through the drawer in the kitchen underneath where Mom keeps her to-do notebook and found a few pictures.

'Gosh.' She had my eyebrows. She looked a lot like me, granted, we were like six in the picture, but still...But her face was fuller than mine, and she was a couple inches taller. Her hair was straight—no bangs—and coffee bean brown. I was in the picture too, with curly hair and, peculiarly, I was skinny to the bone and ratty like an aged Barbie doll. Why didn't I remember my childhood?

My friends and I were trying to take a picture on our phones of the photograph—to keep as evidence. (My friends were only there because they liked pretending to be detectives.)

And with that, my dream ended while we were trying to get a good angle in the light.

If We're Being Honest: Part One

Loving him is like
Chocolate
On Valentine's Day:
Expensive
Overrated
And extremely necessary.

If We're Being Honest: Part Two

Loving him is like
Smoking stardust:
Suffocating
Intoxicating
And magical.

Love

The only emotional experience beyond ourselves, upon which the human race is dependent. In other words, Aidan.

Two Halves

December 21, 2017

2017
Has seen
This acorn grow into a mighty tree
Sprouting leaves
And
Giggles and shy smiles
Fights and awkward hugs
Heavy breaths down my neck
Minty lips exploring your face
Heavy words and I-love-yous.

Like stars bursting at the treetops of the sky
My heart has swelled to twice its size
And I get a little chill
When I say your name
Oh, your name
What once used to contain just five letters
Now entails a thousand words
Each one of them flickering in my mind like small flames
As your image inspires so many memories.

I once saw a story
About ancient Greece
Which said that
Humans once
Had four arms and four legs
But Zeus.

Fearing humans would grow too powerful
Split them into two arms, two legs
Thus, deterring them from their conquer of the
Galaxy, instead sentencing them to
A life of looking and longing and loving
Searching for their other half.

2017
Saw two halves become one.

Touch

December 21, 2017

It’s the
Pins and needles
Cascading down my spine
And through my veins
When you touch me.

Like a fire
Zipping along my skin
From shoulders to legs
Down my body and
Each nerve is being reborn
Invigorated
By the scent of your presence
And each of the hairs on my arms
Stand on end
My senses fully alert
As you trace your fingers
Down my back.

And something like this—

This feeling of flying
While still tied to the ground
Anchored in someone’s arms
Must be
Magic.

365 Good Days

December 21, 2017

Our first 365 days together have been
An incredibly lengthy playlist of
Love songs
A year's worth of three-minute intervals
Each melody
Sending sparks off in my brain
Like candlelight flickering with
Every achingly beautiful memory of your presence
And I get chills just thinking about you
While Staring out the car window and thinking.

Knowing that it doesn't matter
Whether it's January or June or September
Wednesday or Friday or Sunday
All I need to do
Is wake up in the morning knowing
That today is another day
I get to spend with you in my life
For that reason alone
Today will be a good day
So, thank you for 365 good days, my love.

One Entire Year with You

December 30, 2017

To: Kelly; Love: Aidan

When we first met, all I could think about you was "Wow! There's this girl in my History class with some hot legs!" But as the year went on, I got to know you better, and I started to talk to you more often during lunch and took extra care to compliment you when I thought you looked pretty. Yet, at that point, I had never anticipated that we would end up together. After all, how could such a goddess want to be with me—that loud, annoying kid in History?

But then, I fell in love with your voice. I loved to hear it, and making you talk became a game I could play with myself. At this point, I really wanted to ask you out, for you always filled my head in the shower and my dreams at night. Still, I made the decision not to, because basketball season was coming up, and I wouldn't have any free time, plus I still didn't really think I had a chance with you.

Then, after school, on the last day before Christmas vacation, you asked me out. Holy cats!!!

Six months later, I was so in love with you that I could barely even imagine what life was like before you came along...and I really, really tried to, too...I tried to remember what numbness felt like. But I realized that those six months had been the first time in my life when I had been able to FEEL for an extended period of time. You make me happy, and you make me sad, excited, exhausted, trusting, and terrified. You allow me to feel things, and you should know that no matter what emotion I'm feeling toward you in a given moment, it's always better than none at all. It's better than being numb. And to this day, I continue to feel things for you.

Wow, it's been a whole year, Love Bug. When I met you for the first time, I didn't know anything beyond the surface of your brown hair and hot legs. I didn't know about your struggle with anorexia, I didn't know how much I loved the ring of your voice, and I certainly didn't know you would be the one I'd fall head over heels for. I didn't know how strong and brave you are. I didn't know about the freckles on your collarbone or the perfect shape of your little white teeth. I didn't know that your laugh would send sparks down my spine. I didn't know I would fall so in love with you that it would bring new meaning to the expression 'I'd give an arm for you,' because I genuinely would.

In one year, I have learned all of this about you, and much more. I learned that our love is strong enough to withstand any argument, and I learned that there no way in Heaven nor Hell I could ever, ever, ever stop falling for you. Over 365 days later, and I'm still in a free fall...and you know the best part? I doubt there will be a floor for me to hit. You will forever be my first and my only.

I love you more than I could have ever thought possible; you are my entire world, Love Bug.

Love,

Aidan.

One Beautiful Human

He took a paintbrush to the sky
And filled it up with stars
He made my world a little brighter
And basically, stole my heart.

He was my midnight text
My *'please stay'* and *'I love you'*
He was my hand to hold
And chest to lay on; He was
All I needed all in one

One beautiful human.

You

November 20, 2017

You make my heart melt and my stomach drop and my yes tear up a little bit with all the glorious memories of you: The way you bite your lip when you're concentrating. The sexy way your headphones drip out the neck of your black sweatshirt. Sounds of your heart beating when I lay on your chest. Music through the phone when you call me up and play guitar for me. A lack of air in my lungs when you squeeze me extra tight and bury my face in your chest. How I am hopelessly addicted to your touch and the sound of your voice. The contagious smile always on your face that spreads like wildfires. When your whole face lights up when you have a new idea. The way you listen to the same music I'd always teased my mom for listening to. Tasting you on my lips even after we've parted.

Melt My Heart

December 31, 2017

You're the most lovable
Most sweetest
Person
In the whole wide world and
This is why I love you:
You never cease to
Melt my soul like liquid dreams.
You make my heart laugh and cry and yearn and
Beat and just well up inside
Like one big giant firework…
Just by being in it.

A Love

He was made of stardust
And people say
He could talk to the moon
And would swim in the sky.

He also met a girl
She was from Earth
And he stole her heart
He kept it safe.

He did not just give her
The world
But he showed her
The entire galaxy.

The One

December 31, 2017

Bajillions of humans in this world
But
I found *you*.

Recovery

The healing. A very, very, very slow process of rebuilding and coming back to life. Can refer to the healing of a physical wound, like physical therapy for injured athletes or a mental recovery—PTSD, rape, etc.

Insignificance

January 24, 2016

I just realized something that I hadn't before. 'SMALL' (too short, too skinny)…does not equal 'INSIGNIFICANT' (lesser value, unimportant, a joke, not enough)…

To the average onlooker, these words may have no relation at all. They may have different meaning or uses. But if you relate to the statement above, we are probably very similar, and you should take notes on the rest of this essay…

It genuinely breaks my heart when people comment on my size, and specifically my height—a huge insecurity of mine—because I always subconsciously translate that into *'insignificant.'* Of course, it is likely that nobody is *'trying'* to say that I'm 'insignificant'; they are probably just noticing my petiteness. Yet, I reason that my slight figure only amplifies my 5' stature because it makes me look like a 16-year-old girl's head sitting on a 12-year-old's body. Is that attractive? I guess it depends who you ask.

If I were to be heavier at the same height, it would probably make me look more my age, but that would also amplify how short I am because I'd look stubby. Is that attractive? I guess it depends who you ask.

But now, maybe you see; I can't win either way. Honestly, if someone thought the world of me, and thought I was a strong and healthy person, and thought I was beautiful, yet also happen to respectfully point out that I'm vertically challenged, I wouldn't be phased. That's why it doesn't bothers me when Aidan, for example, comments on how small I am compared to him—a full 12 inches taller than me. But when a random classmate or even a friend of mine—who thinks well of me—laughs at my height or picks me up and won't put me down, then I don't know whether or not they are making fun of my existence along with my height! I wouldn't know because they never *'told me out loud'* that they think I am a good person! They only told me about my *'height,'* which is what I am already aware of! I find it frustrating how people so often feel the need to remind me of my size as if I didn't know already. Can any other of you petite ladies out there relate? *'Hello! This is my body, I am completely aware of all my features, and I don't need to be reminded of the less desirable ones!'*

This is what I have figured out: *'the way I say things to myself. Don't you get it?' I interpret other people calling me "small" as if they were calling me "insignificant" because that is the way I say it to myself.*

Only recently did I realize that this is unique to me, normal people don't translate these words the same way as I do, and that I have never in my life met somebody as cruel as the voice inside my head. I hear that's pretty universal, though, we're all running from our own demons.

When someone in the hallway plays on my insecurities by calling me out for my height or another physical feature, it takes me right to a flashback of having a *'fat attack,'* alone in my room. *'Ed'* ruthlessly castigating me for being fat, short, insignificant, worthless, and a huge joke to humanity. *'I know,'* I'm so dramatic!

Human Emotion

February 13, 2017

People have so many differences: race, gender, social class, religion, age, sexuality, ethnicity, intellectual ability, personality, and literally everything that makes us unique. But we have one thing in common, that is far, far more important than anything that could ever classify us, it is that **we are all human.**

It doesn't matter where in the world we live; we all experiment the same basic life events: Friendship, puberty, romance, loss, etc. At the end of the day, we all experience the same emotions: pleasure, longing, lust, sadness, grief, guilt, excitement, hopelessness, joy, compassion, sympathy, anxiety, etc. Does any of this sound familiar? If they do, it's because you are *'human'*!

Fun fact: I am a human. I have been around for 16 years now. I have experienced several emotions, in as many different shades as there are colors on earth, and not just the few that humans can see. Honestly, I've endured a shit ton of emotion and fought very hard to get through it. People think emotions are for sappy people. But they can leave you feeling like you've just run a marathon. For me, I always feel like I'm drowning. Managing emotions should be an Olympic sport. But something I have realized is that the only thing worse than excruciating emotion is none at all. You'd think it would be peaceful—having a quiet mind for once. But it's not all that great. When you can't feel or care about anything at all, that's called depression. I know because I have it.

Emotion is a beautiful thing and should be felt. *'Emotion is human.'* See what I did there? *Whether it's the emotion that makes us human or that being human makes us emotional, I am not quite sure.*

So many people in today's society are AFRAID of their emotions and don't even know it. *Why the fuck do you think so many genocides have happened?!'* Because people are AFRAID!!! I have endured countless internal genocides. I struggled for months during recovery, trying to understand how my heart can break in the same place every time. *'Why doesn't the feeling get old? Why do I have fat attacks over and over again?'* Lindsay explained it. ' It's what's behind the fear that changes, which is why fear is able to attack so many times without growing dull. For me, in my personal struggle, I know that fat attacks are triggered by outside stressors, like boy-drama or school anxiety, that is then channeled into self-hate and body shaming. Similarly, each genocide was born from very different yet similarly stressful and intense situations within a particular country. Of course, they did, because they all took place on different time periods and different places. But how individuals experience the same human emotions regardless of differences, such as age, nationality, religion, and time period, each genocide was rooted in the emotion known as fear!

I could *force* people to feel their emotions. Then, maybe, people will come to terms with their emotion a little bit more. Because as I have learned (the hard way!), emotions do not disappear. If they did, humanity would not have made it this far. Not a chance.

I argue that if humans cannot openly and efficiently process their emotions on an individual level, we have no hope for the future, regarding complex politics and economics. Without emotion—that tired but calm feeling in the morning after crying yourself to sleep the night prior, and that deep breath of ocean air if you're lucky enough to smell it, the way you watch the waves slosh over each other in unorganized harmony and somehow in that moment when the sun hits your shoulders it feels like a hug from behind, and you know that everything will be okay—we lose all that which connects us with the earth and the natural world we live in. *Emotion reminds people of their humanity*. At the end of the day, we are all human, and as a species of animals, we mustn't pretend we are robots in this industrial first world society.

For the very good of an individual's peace of mind, spiritual well-being, and physical health, I suggest that each person makes it a priority to spend at least 20 minutes out in nature per day. Now, I'm not going all *'Walden-Pond'* on you, so don't worry, but I say this because I have walked both the length of New Zealand and the length of India all on a one-mile neighborhood called Acorn Street. It took me about 4 years. But as often as possible, I make a point to walk to the end of this street and back, for a total of two miles, always just around sunset. I listen to music and drink up my data plan, listening to YouTube music for free, but it's okay. On these walks, I find that I am naturally drawn into my emotions, alone with myself and the sidewalk and trees; this is where I not only have some of my best ideas, but also my deepest realizations about myself. It is important to find somewhere peaceful—be it on a walk, in the forest, or just in your bedroom with a warm cup of tea—to just be alone and spend some quality time with yourself. Believe it or not, it is unlikely that you know as much about yourself as you think you do. I sure didn't. You think this book wrote itself?!

I am a believer in life. But in the depths of my ED and negative emotion, admittedly, I wasn't always such a fan. My therapist, Lindsay, says, "You can't have the rainbow without the rain." And I fought really hard through my storm to get to my rainbow. And now, things are looking up for me. I am a believer in BETTER lives. I am a believer in facing emotion and *'accepting'* fear.

The Uncomfortable

July 4, 2017

It's when I'm on a run and in the last stretch of sidewalk, one more house before mine. My mind yells at me: *finish strong! Go as hard as you can on this one! Sprint to the finish! Push it! Push it! Push it!* So, I start going faster and faster and keep pushing until I am going hard enough that the pushes become smaller and more difficult. This is when I must choose between uncharted territory—go harder than I've ever pushed—or slow down and ease my way back into a jog, making excuses as I go, is the moment when I have to make decisions. Do I go into uncharted territory—'The Uncomfortable?' Why is it uncomfortable, you may ask? Because it's *'unknown.'* People are terrified of the unknown, which is why most people who push themselves into it—dare to be vulnerable and raw and uncomfortable—win awards and praise from the world. Olympic athletes strive for the uncomfortable because they know that's where they'll grow. Why do they grow in 'The Uncomfortable,' you may ask? 'The Uncomfortable' is equivalent to 'The Unknown' because you don't know what'll happen after it. Then, once you finish your final push, that future is met, and it's *'not unknown anymore.'* So next time when you reach that point, you can push through it and on to new unknown territory, and so on! Let me give you an example: I choose to go for the unknown. I push my legs and tighten my core and brain and body pulses in synchronously with the air and ground itself. The wind rushes past my ears, and I have trouble focusing my eyes on the ground. I don't know whether I'm going to trip on a pothole, slip in the sand, collapse in my driveway, have my heart stop because I pushed my weak body too far…I don't know. It's not just in sports, either. In theater and music, when you get on stage, that's a risk as well. When you pour your heart into the lyrics of a song and sing your deepest darkest secrets into a microphone for the whole world to hear, that is vulnerable. It is unknown, because you don't know if your song is good or what people will think when they hear. Just think about how many things are unknown and how humanity fittingly deems them uncomfortable…like death. Our brains physically cannot comprehend death because a dead person never lives to tell the story…and it shall remain forever unknown. What about relationships? Love? The list goes on. Moral of the story is, we must push ourselves to 'The Uncomfortable' to be great. Not everyone who does gets awards or even wins. But it's worth trying. If we're going to be human, then, heck, I want to be human all the way. Be angry, sad, talented, awkward, smart, gross, passionate, uncomfortable, and you will be beautiful. I promise. Be it because that's what it means when they say, *'Be yourself.' 'Yourself'* is better than *'beautiful'*; it is *real.*

Music

July 4, 2017

There are different kinds of days.

Sometimes, the music sounds good, and sometimes it doesn't. Not necessarily according to happy or sad days, but it's similar to how when you open the fridge, sometimes you don't want anything even though you're hungry, and sometimes the same food you eat every day looks absolutely delicious, and you can't decide what to have.

The music sounds good today.

I don't know why, but it just feels like that kind of day when all the old 2012 pop hits on my phone, that have been there forever and that I've heard a thousand times, all sound almost new again. I can put it on shuffle and not have to skip any songs, which is a rarity for me.

Today is a good day. I can feel it…
I can hear it.

Recovery Part 4

Because it didn't work the first or the second or the third time.

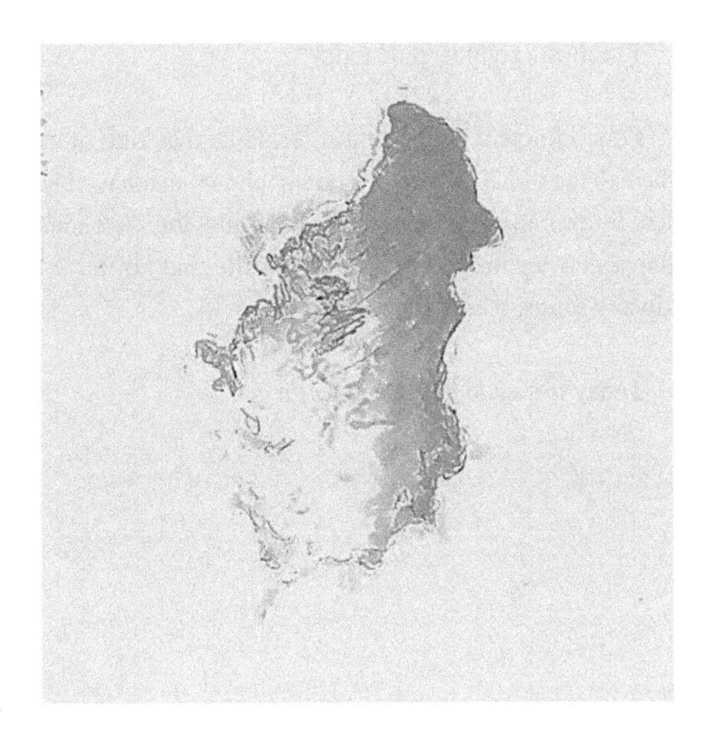

A Quote

December 8, 2016

"You know you're getting better
When you look in the mirror
And
See a *sick* person
Rather than a *bad* one."

— John, *Improbable Players*

A Note About Mental Illness

December 14, 2017

I think
People wouldn’t suffer as much
If
They didn’t have to do it in **silence**.

Crayons

December 24, 2017

There is a variety
Of flavors
In this world
The white and black
The gray
And then there are humans
With color
But I wish to propose an alternative:
Brown
I wish to live
So colorfully
That my soul may look like
A painter's pallet
Red, green, blue, pink, yellow
Mashed into one brown, vomit
Like dirty
Looking blob
I want every wavelength
Of the visible spectrum
To course through my veins
Like electricity
Like Christmas lights or candles
My heart flickering to the beat of its
Own drum
Like a thousand orchestras
In Symphony Hall
And
I wish to smell, hear, and taste

Every hue of the
Rainbow
I wish to live so colorfully
So musically, vividly, vibrantly
That I may never even think
To look down
And see how ugly I am.

You Can't Have a Rainbow Without a Little Rain

February 15, 2017

I am in my rainbow now, and I worry
That something will jinx me and life will soon slap me in the face
Because
That's what people say always happens:
Just when you think everything's fine, something goes wrong.
But you know what? Lindsay is right:
I have worked hard to be here
It didn't just happen
I suffered a lot and fought very hard for this rainbow
I deserve it.

Three years ago, two years ago, one year ago
I didn't see the rainbow ahead
It was raining and
It was raining hard
For a long time, and
I honestly figured it would rain until I drowned in it.

But now
There is a beautiful rainbow
With some mists, showers, and clouds occasionally hazing the sky
But the colors are bright.

I now have everything
That I wanted.

A year ago
Because I worked my butt off to get them.

Life isn't going to slap me in the face
Just for the sake of having something go wrong
But no
I *am* going to be successful and do well in life
Because
I am going to work for it
Just as I did for everything else.

Head Above Water

December 14, 2017

Oh my actual
Freaking
Goodness.

What an incredibly
Liberating
Feeling it is
To live again.

It starts with a sudden gasp for air
As your head
Unexpectedly
Bobs above the surface of the water
You've been drowning in for the past few years
And
It's funny because this kind of miraculous recovery
Tends to happen
Right after
You feel your lungs on fire
Stinging intensely as water rushes into them
When you were sure you were done for, for good.

But that was the point
You experienced pain because
You finally stopped treading water
Yes, you naturally and immediately began to sink once you stopped

But stopping is also what later allowed you to escape
From the mighty waters
And scramble, thrashing, searching for land.

And the air tasted so sweet
Like breathing in a field of carnations
Or diving into a pitcher of maple syrup
And oh honey
It was well worth the swim.

And now
I could drown a thousand
Oceans
With my thoughts
My powerful, positive thoughts.

Acorn Street: Part 8: Golden Skies

So many evenings of pink sunsets, my favorite color, the kind that make you stop in the middle of your run to take pictures. Also, the glowing orange kind, the kind so orange that you must stop your conversation or stroll, and just take a breath and appreciate how orange it is. To be honest, I really, really hate the color orange, so much so that my boyfriend literally threw out his only orange shirt when we started dating just to be careful. But that one burning sunset on Golden Run is the only color of orange I secretly love. Some days, it's the kind of weather that sets the sky on fire and turns the clouds pink. Other times, the last breath of daylight kisses the trees and makes it look like they are on fire, and the clouds are the smoke. Either way, it's the kind of sunset where I don't even mind that I was all the way on the other side of the street, a mile away from home, when the sky faded to darkness. Because I get a better view of the colors from the other side of the street.

It was worth having to feel my way home.

Author's Note

This book was named after an incredibly inspiring TED Talk I watched on YouTube during the few first months of writing this book. It is entitled *'Eating Disorders from the Inside Out by Laura Hill,'* filmed at TEDx Columbus. I'm the type of sappy person that spends their free time watching TED talks. I can affirm to the best of my judgment that this is the most accurate and most thoughtful explanation of anorexia I have ever heard. Bonus: she's a doctor. I highly recommend anybody with a child, friend, or loved one who is suffering from an eating disorder to check it out.

One of the two main goals I have for this book is to make people *'understand.'* Public education about mental illness is important to me because my own parents come from a generation which barely even knew what mental illness was.

The first step to overcoming mental illness—on a small scale and worldwide—is talking about it! And it's not as hard as you'd think; every human knows the feelings of guilt, nervousness, fear, irritability, loss, etc. Why is love so relatable if not everybody has actually experienced it? Because it's a feeling! You just know. Even when you've never felt it, humans can perceive emotions accordingly. It's called 'empathy.' My goal is that anyone who reads this book can walk away with a basic understanding of and empathy towards the concept of mental noise, even if only a little. In a society that refuses to speak up about mental health, I have attempted to start that conversation.

Going off that note, to those who know *'exactly'* what I've been through, and for those who have experienced anything similar, such as depression, anxiety, bipolar disorder, etc., my dearest hope is that you may find comfort in this book. Not comfort that everything is fine, for there is no escape from the very real world in which your brain lives. But I want you to know that you are not alone, and that those thoughts are not unique to you. Just because nobody talks about them doesn't mean that nobody feels them. You are not alone.

CPSIA information can be obtained
at www.ICGtesting.com
Printed in the USA
BVHW041059211219
567438BV00018B/762/P